75 DAYS OF JO

To Aunt Harriet,
Thank you <u>so</u> much
for all the support.
Love,
Jess

J M

75 DAYS OF JO

JESSICA MCCARTER PONTILLO

NEW DEGREE PRESS
75 DAYS OF JO

ISBN   978-1-63676-569-3   *Paperback*
       978-1-63676-163-3   *Kindle Ebook*
       978-1-63676-165-7   *Ebook*

To my friends, my family, and my Bretty.
I don't know where I'd be without you.

CONTENTS

———

DAY 1

CHAPTER 1

———

Today is the day I will officially move into Pennington State College. I don't think I've ever been so terrified.

Summer flew by, just as everyone told me it would. It's my last summer before college—before leaving my family and hometown of Drew, the very quaint suburban New York town I lived in for eighteen years.

Two months ago, I graduated from high school, class of 2020! I can't believe how quickly it flew by. I remember my first day of so vividly, sitting in the auditorium with the other freshmen—all nervous and excited for what was to come. We were all so young back then, even though we all felt pretty mature. All the girls had gotten their eyebrows done for the first time and the boys shaved the hair on their faces they *swore* was there. Flash forward four years and all those kids are going to college. Including me.

As I'm lying in bed slowly waking up and trying to wrap my head around this realization, I hear my mom calling.

"Jo!"

I take a big deep breath, trying to calm myself down before throwing the covers off and making my way downstairs.

"Jo, you're not even dressed? We have to leave in an hour!"

I take hold of the wood banister at the top of the stairs. Our home is a five-bedroom house complete with white siding, red front door, and navy blue shutters. Very quintessential suburbia. You know the type; that's my house.

I feel a twinge of guilt as I see Mom rushing around the living room, making sure all my things are packed.

"Mom, I got this!" I tell her as I grab the bulk pack of toilet paper from her tiny frame. "Remind me why I'm packing so much toilet paper? I'll be in a dorm with communal bathrooms!" I can't help but start laughing; it feels like a cathartic release on such a life-changing day.

"Good point. I'll send you with twenty-five rolls instead of forty-five." Mom sticks her tongue out at me and continues to triple-check the bags we packed last night.

I'm emotional as I watch her. I'm not going to be living with my parents or brothers anymore, our perfect family of five, the people I love most in the world. Even though I know it will interrupt her methodical bag checking, I walk up behind her and give her a big hug.

I feel her stiffen and then relax. Mom's face turns from "mom on a mission" to "momma bear comforting her cub" in a second. It's one of the reasons I love her; she's always worn so many hats to be what my brothers and I needed her to be at any given moment. Thinking of it brings tears to my eyes.

"Hey, Jo, honey, what's going on?" She wipes the tears from my cheeks.

"I just...I'm just going to miss you so much, Mom."

"Ha! Where was this Jo two years ago when you wanted nothing to do with me? Huh?" Mom smiles warmly and pokes my stomach.

"Come on, Mom. I've already apologized for my angsty teenage years."

"I know, I know. But that doesn't mean I won't bring it up every chance I get. I wouldn't be a mom if I didn't."

"You're supposed to be comforting me because I'm sad, remember?"

She takes my hand in hers and leads us to the couch. "That's right. Well, let me ask you this, do you not want to go away to school?"

"Not exactly. I'm just nervous about this whole thing. I've never even gone to sleep-away camp and now I'm moving to a different state—to a place where I don't know anyone. Plus, I won't be with you and Dad and the stupid boys anymore." Any composure I had gained is now completely lost. Who knew I would cry over not living with my brothers anymore? They're annoying most of the time.

My mom starts rubbing my back, something she's always done to comfort me. "I know it's scary, Jo. Think of it this way: it's a once-in-a-lifetime opportunity! To start fresh, meet new people, experience new things, and find who you are."

"I guess..."

"You're Jo Prescott." Mom sweeps back my long, sandy-blond hair and looks into my deep green eyes. "I know you'll make this a great experience for yourself. You've got this." She gives me an encouraging smile. "Now wipe the tears off your face and get your butt in the shower, Jelly. If you still want to go to school, we're going to need to leave in, oh my goodness, forty-five minutes!"

My parents have called me Jelly since I was a little girl. Not sure where it came from and, to be honest, I don't even remember when they started calling me by that nickname. My parents are the only ones who call me by this, so it always makes me feel special.

Even though I'm still nervous as hell, I don't want to worry Mom any longer. I paste the best smile I can muster on my face.

Mom gives me one last hug before she pushes me upstairs to get ready.

I try my best to relax during my twenty-minute scalding hot shower and think about literally anything else besides the feeling in the pit of my stomach. It's like I'm on a roller coaster going down the biggest drop, but the end hasn't come yet. No matter what I do, I can't seem to shake it.

"Jo! We leave in ten!" My ears hurt from Mom's yelling. For a small lady, she has a big voice.

I rush to get dressed in the dark green PSC shirt I bought at orientation and my favorite white jean shorts. I brush a little mascara on my eyelashes—the most I ever do, since I'm not very good at makeup—and lace up my Keds. I take a quick look at myself in the mirror. It's strange wearing a PSC shirt on move-in day...will it make me seem like a dork? Dad insisted I wear it; he thinks I'll stand out if I'm *not* in PSC green. All my other clothes are packed, so I don't really have other options anyway.

As I'm about to leave my childhood bedroom, I do probably the worst thing anyone in my emotional state could do—take one last look.

My room looks the same on the surface—my bed with its lilac comforter, my mahogany desk, my double-door closet, and bookshelf—it's all still there but it's different. I've packed my favorite books, most of my clothes, and my family photos to take with me. This isn't really my room anymore. Tears spring to my eyes again. It's time to leave. I say a silent good-bye to my room, turn off my lights, and head downstairs, knowing it will be the last time for a while.

* * *

I'm about to slide into the back of my family car when I feel a hand catch my arm. It's my dad.

"Hey, Jelly, is everything okay? Mom said you were upset." The concern in his eyes almost brings me to tears. I look down at my feet to compose myself. I need to stop the waterworks.

"I'm okay, Dad, just nerves I think."

Dad wraps his arms around me in a tight embrace that immediately catches me off guard. Dad's usually Mr. Stoic and often keeps to himself. He's one of my favorite people in the world.

"Jo, everything will be okay. Sure, college will be an adjustment. There will be times when you are frustrated and maybe even lonely. But remember it's only temporary. Sometimes we have to go through something challenging or uncomfortable to grow. All I ask is that you give yourself time...Time to adjust. Time to let this experience be great." He pulls away from our embrace and gives me one of his rare crinkle-eyed smiles.

I nod and wrap my arms around him for one more hug.

* * *

I know I won't be able to hold back more tears if I have to talk to my parents during the car ride, so as soon as I get in the backseat, I put my headphones in and play my Alternative Punk playlist—very apt for my current moodiness—and turn it up to drown out any other noise. As Good Charlotte croons in my ears, I try not think about how my life will change in just a few hours.

I let my thoughts wander as clothes, bedding, books, and much more are piled around me. My mind lands on my most positive PSC memory to date: the day I got my acceptance letter.

It started off as any other uneventful winter school day. I sipped on my morning earl grey tea and waited for homeroom to start, not even fully awake when I heard a conversation between a few of the girls behind me.

"Did you see Angela's post last night? She got into PSC!"

"I didn't even think she wanted to go there."

"Not sure, but I guess this means the big colleges are starting to send out their letters."

I didn't really hear anything after "Angela got her acceptance from PSC." My mind raced. Where was my letter? Did I get in? Would I find out today? Why didn't I study harder for the SATs? Ugh, I really don't want to go to my safety school! For the rest of the day, those exact thoughts looped through my mind. I couldn't focus on anything except that damned letter.

The crazy thing? I hadn't even known what PSC was until a few months ago. After what felt like a hundred schools, I was convinced I would never have that feeling. The "Oh, my God, this is the school for me" feeling people talk about. All the colleges seemed to be selling the same thing—lots of clubs, great academics, and some "quirk" that made their school special. One school we toured boasted of having the best dining hall in the entire US. Another school tried to sell us on the fact that they had a "couch club." I guess college students like sitting on couches as a collective? Not sure, but I wasn't into it. I didn't know what I was looking for, but I knew those schools just weren't it.

By some miracle or twist of fate, the very last school was the one I fell in love with. As soon as I stepped foot on PSC's campus for a tour, I had *the feeling*. The shiver down my spine, butterflies in my stomach feeling. Sure, the tour guide talked about clubs on campus, great academics, and mentioned some quirky things, but it was different here. The school spirit was unlike anything I had ever seen before. Throughout the entire PSC tour, students would shout at us "PSC is the place to be!" or "Go here, you'll have the time of your life!" After about the tenth time of that happening, our tour guide told us it was part of the unofficial PSC bucket list to shout at the campus tour groups. It was a school full of people who were excited to be where they were. That's what I wanted.

There I was, on pins and needles, desperate for school to end so I could get home to check the mail. Finally, three o'clock came and I left school as soon as that closing bell rang.

I pulled into my driveway and rushed to the mailbox. No mail. Mom must have already brought it inside. Crap. I didn't want anyone to see my letter before I did! I ran inside to the kitchen counter. Rifled through the mail. No college letters!

Mom found me acting like a madwoman. She started to laugh. "Looking for something?" She said with a hint of humor in her voice.

I tried to act casual. "Nope, just thought I might have some mail today."

"I'm sorry, Jo, but I didn't see anything in there for you."

I tried not to look upset as I turned around and went upstairs to my room. It's my own personal belief that no one should ever be in anything but sweats and T-shirts in their own home. My routine after school was always to head directly to my room to change out of my jeans and bra and into the comfy stuff.

In my room, there was a big envelope with the PSC emblem in the top left corner. Just sitting on my bed.

I ripped open the letter.

"Dear Jo, we are pleased to inform you..."

And that's when I lost my shit. I threw my hands up in the air and screamed at the top of my lungs, *"I'm in!"*

Mom ran in to join me. We hugged and jumped up and down for about five minutes. My younger brother, Ollie, popped into my room, said "Congrats," and scurried off, probably to re-read his favorite *Game of Thrones* book.

That night, Dad brought home flowers for me and a pizza for everyone to celebrate.

* * *

I'm jostled out of my reverie when Dad says, "We're almost there!"

I notice the highway exit sign that says PSC is five miles north. Just like that, my nerves are back in full force. My breath quickens, and I'm about a minute away from asking Dad to pull over so I can puke on the side of the highway. My hands are clammy and I can't seem to think straight. Is this really happening? Can I do this?

CHAPTER 2

We take the PS7C exit and, for a split second, my nerves subside and excitement takes over as the campus comes into view. Seeing the buildings and the huge Pennington State College sign reminds me of the feeling I had the day of my tour. Hundreds of students and their parents mill about campus, unpacking cars and moving into dorms. All freshmen move in on the same day, so I'm assuming most of these students are first years like me.

A student in a bright green Welcome Committee shirt stands in the parking lot. She greets us, "Hi, folks! What dorm are you trying to get to?"

"Hi, there, we're going to Graham." Dad tries but fails to sound as upbeat as this energetic student. I try my best not to laugh at his expense.

"Ah, Lackawanna community! I lived there my freshmen year." She looks through the car window to me and says, "You're going to love it!"

I give her a big smile. "I hope so, I've heard great things." I hadn't actually heard much about Lackawanna, but I didn't want to be rude.

She looks back to Dad and says, "You're just going to drive straight and turn left on Lackawanna Street. There will be thirty-minute parking for you to unpack your stuff. Once you're done unpacking, please park your car in one of the designated campus lots."

My dad nods and, to my complete embarrassment, answers, "Thanks. Let's go, PSC!"

I put my hand over my face and sink lower into my seat so I don't have to see the welcome girl's face.

It's pure chaos in my dorm community. There must be thousands of freshmen in these five dorm buildings alone. The buildings look fairly old from the outside—made of brick with one window per room by the looks of it. Many of the windows have box fans propped against them or Greek letters taped to the inside of the window for passersby to see.

All the dorms at PSC are named after counties in Pennsylvania. My internet research said Lackawanna houses students from all years, which, if I'm being honest, intimidates the hell out of me. I had applied to be in the freshmen community called Montgomery, even though by all accounts it's the worst place to live—co-ed bathrooms, a musty smell that never quite goes away no matter how many times it's cleaned, the worst dining hall, and the smallest (and oldest) rooms on campus. But I wanted the true freshman experience, surrounded by students new to PSC. Montgomery is supposedly *wild*. Lots of partying, noise 24/7, and vomit surrounding the grounds every Thursday through Sunday.

The last two years of high school, my friends and I started drinking occasionally but never anything too serious. We weren't popular, so we never got invited to the cool parties. We had a group of about ten friends who would get together, make a bonfire in a backyard in the summer, and drink until the mosquitoes were so bad we had to go inside. I was just too responsible to go much further than that. Maybe it was a sign from the universe that Montgomery would be too crazy for me; maybe Lackawanna would be a better fit.

As we pull up to Graham and grab a parking space, Mom says enthusiastically, "This building looks nice!" I can tell she's trying to sound upbeat for me, but Graham looks no different than the other buildings in Lackawanna.

Dad, as efficient and eager as ever, hops out of the car and finds one of the school's moving-in carts. He starts unloading the car immediately, Mom turns to the backseat, and we exchange the "he's crazy" look. I can't help but giggle.

"Why don't you grab a few of the lighter things back there, Jo? Pass me some too while you're at it," Mom says.

I spot the toilet paper and make a mental note to hide it in the bottom of the cart on our next trip so no one will see it. I think I'm probably the only student living on campus who packed that much toilet paper...or any toilet paper at all for that matter.

I pass Mom my comforter and I grab a pillow and a small duffle bag that has my sheets and pillowcases in it. This is probably good for now.

Mom and I get out of the car and she yells to Dad, "Harry, we're going to get Jo's room key! See you in there!"

Dad doesn't even pop his head up. When he's in the zone, he's in the zone.

* * *

The propped-open door to Graham welcomes us. It's a beautiful day and the warm breeze gently flows into the lobby. Right when we walk in, we're stopped by a long folding table, behind which sits two students, a boy and a girl wearing the same bright green welcome shirts as the chipper traffic director.

The boy says, "Hi, I'm Matt. Welcome to Graham Hall! Name and dorm number?"

It takes me a minute to comprehend what's going on because I can't stop staring at this boy. Dark brown hair, tan skin, hazel eyes, a beautiful smile, and muscular arms straining his welcome shirt. Damn, this boy is hot.

Mom must have caught me staring because she gently kicks my calf. I wince. So much for playing it cool.

"Um. Hi. Jo Prescott. Room 409...you know, like the song?" *Oh, my God, why did I say that? No one my age would get that reference!* Embarrassment washes over me, and I'm sure my face is a bright shade of red.

Hot Boy Matt responds with a laugh and sings a line from the song before saying, "Yes, the Beach Boys!"

He must see my shock. "An oldie but a goodie, at least that's what my parents say. They used to play the Beach Boys all the time. 409 was one of my favorites. So catchy." Matt rubs the back of his neck, like maybe he's a little shy too?

"My parents did too! It felt like some weird twist of fate that I got room 409." I smile at Matt. He smiles back.

I'm not sure how many moments go by before the girl sitting next to him says, "Here's your room key! Just go down the hall and elevators are to your right."

Mom and I wave goodbye to them and go on our way.

Mom smirks and whispers, "He was cute!"

I roll my eyes like I don't care, but I seriously hope I see Matt again...and soon.

* * *

I push the elevator button and while we wait, I glance at the bulletin board to my right, which is covered in neon fliers. Most are for campus clubs, with some welcome notes from the resident assistants. My favorite sign is a bright pink one that says *Please Do Not Spit in the Elevator.* I snap a pic of it and chuckle to myself. Is this what college will be like? When the elevator arrives, to our pleasant surprise, there's no spit in it.

* * *

As we walk down the fourth floor hallway, a lot of girls have their doors propped open. I start to feel a pit at the bottom of my stomach. Propping open dorm doors seems like this big signal telling everyone you're putting yourself out there. The pressure begins to weigh on me as that nagging, insecure voice in my head starts up again. *Will people like me? Is anyone else nervous at all?* I try my best to push these thoughts away as I wipe my clammy hands on my shorts in a futile attempt to dry them.

Room 409's door is wide open, like so many others. My roommate, Becky, who I've only texted a few times, lies on her bed, scrolling through her phone. I tentatively knock.

She jumps up and immediately hugs me. With a big smile, she says, "Hi, Jo, it's great to finally meet you!" She seems very warm and welcoming.

I smile back. "Hi, Becky, it's great to meet you too! This is my mom."

"Hi, Mrs. Prescott!" Becky gives Mom a hug too.

I think Mom is startled. She's not really a hugger. She smiles nervously as Becky pulls away.

From our texts, I learned Becky is from Pennsylvania. She grew up in a small town called Clearville, where she lives on a farm with her mom and siblings. She's tall and thin (she must be 5'10") with long wavy brown hair and big brown eyes. She's beautiful and very fashionable. Her makeup looks like it could have been done by a professional.

I'm pretty much the opposite. I'm very petite, 5'1" on a good day, and have my Italian grandmother's thighs and hips. Becky, an eighteen-year-old who could pass for a twenty-five-year-old model, makes me feel extremely young.

Becky says, "My mom made homemade brownies for us. Please take some. I've already had five today." Please tell me, where does Becky have room for five brownies in her tiny, toned stomach? It takes all of three minutes for me to feel jealous of her, and what's even more depressing is that it's not a record for me. Not even close.

Dad comes in with the huge cart full of my stuff and my attention is no longer on Becky. Dad to the rescue, as always.

Becky took the bed closest to the window, which means I get the bed closest to the door. I'm okay with that because the bed is pushed up against the wall and will be cozy. I start to unpack when I notice my parents edging out of the room.

"We'll go get the next round of stuff. Be back in a few." Dad says.

"Oh, I can come too!" I say, looking for any excuse to leave with my parents. I don't know if I can be alone with Becky just yet—I'll just compare myself to her.

"No, no, you start unpacking." When Becky isn't looking, Mom points to me, then points to Becky, and makes a talking gesture with her hands.

I roll my eyes at her and Dad as they walk away.

What should I even say to her? *How was your summer?* I think she was actually here for the summer. PSC offers summer semester to anyone who wants it. It's a chance to enroll in a few classes before your freshman year to help get acclimated and earn a few credits.

Being anything but casual, I lean against some of my moving boxes and ask, "So did you like your time here this summer, Becky?" *Oh, my goodness, what am I, a parent? Why am I acting so formal?*

Becky's looking at herself in the mirror on the inside of her closet and applying a coat of lip gloss. "It. Was. Amazing. We'd party all night, wake up at noon, go to like one class, and then do it all over again. We even became friends with some of the athletes on campus—they couldn't get enough of me and my friends! It was probably the second best summer of my life."

"Oh, what was the first?" My curiosity is getting the best of me.

"The summer I spent in Italy before my senior year. There's no drinking age there, and I met this really hot guy. Marco. He showed me around, if you know what I mean." Becky winks at me.

I'm pretty sure I do. I nod along, try my best to smile, and continue unpacking my things. I can't believe Becky spent a summer in Italy. The farthest from home I've been is Florida. Not as cool as freakin' Italy! The insecurity I feel toward Becky continues to grow.

Relief washes over me when my parents walk through the door a few minutes later. I honestly have no clue what else to talk about with Becky. It doesn't seem like we have anything in common.

"All right, I don't know about you girls, but I'm starving. This packing and unpacking is really working up my appetite," Mom says.

"I can always eat!" Becky replies. Of course she can.

"It's settled then. Let's go!" Dad exclaims.

To my surprise, as we're leaving the dorm, Dad tries to make conversation with Becky. "So, how do you like PSC? Jo mentioned you were here over the summer?"

"I love it here! I had the best time this summer. Everyone I've met so far is really nice! I got a chance to explore campus and downtown. I've already made two great girlfriends and know where my classes will be." When my parents aren't looking, Becky looks at me and winks.

Who is this girl?

* * *

Dad has to park the car in one of the on-campus lots, so he says he'll meet us at the dining hall.

On our walk there, I notice a lot of students with PSC lanyards around their necks and their dorm keys strung on.

I'm about to say I like the PSC lanyards when Becky says with a laugh, "You can tell who the freshmen are because they wear lanyards around their necks. Kinda lame, if you ask me."

We *are* freshmen, though. The way she says it makes it seem like it's a bad thing. *Mental note: do not wear a lanyard.*

* * *

The dining hall is massive and packed. We pick a table where we can meet after we get our food. Mom and I go together to explore the smorgasbord of options. Excitement washes through me when I notice the soft serve ice cream machine in the corner—my favorite! Then I immediately feel dread... I'm definitely going to gain the freshman fifteen.

"So Becky seems nice," Mom says.

"Yeah, she seems nice enough."

"You don't sound so sure."

I shrug. "I just feel like she's already so comfortable here. And settled. Did you see how many toiletries she had?"

Becky has an entire bin under her bed full of makeup. Every product you could think of. I don't even know what half of it is! She also has a second bin full of hair accessories, including but not limited to: a curling iron, hair straightener, headbands, scrunchies, and a bunch of expensive-looking hair products.

I have one sad, small box: a tube of toothpaste, a toothbrush, a bar of Ivory soap, shampoo and conditioner, my lone eyeliner pencil, and tube of mascara.

"You'll be settled in before you know it." Mom assures me.

I make a face.

"So she got a head start! Don't let it bother you. She was here over the summer when there were only a few hundred people on campus. There are going to be forty thousand people on campus in the next day. It'll be a transition for her too."

Mom is trying to reassure me, but all I hear is "forty thousand people on campus." Holy crap. So many! But Mom's right. It's a new playing field, a fresh start, a new semester. Hope starts to bubble within me.

"You never know, you two may become great friends. Try to keep yourself open to any possibility, Jelly."

I really doubt Becky and I will become good friends, but Mom's right. I should be optimistic. With the biggest smile I can muster, I reply, "I'll try my best, Mom."

Salad has the shortest line, so Mom and I pick that and head to our designated meeting table. Becky is already there, shoveling her hamburger and fries into her mouth. Somehow, she doesn't look like a mess. *How is this possible?* I'd have grease running down my cheek and ketchup on my shirt by now if I were eating that. Mom and I join her, and as I pick at my salad, Dad walks up excitedly.

"Look what I got you!" He opens his hand and there lies a hunter-green PSC lanyard. He puts it over my head. Womp, Womp.

* * *

As the four of us walk back to the dorm, I know the time is coming for Mom and Dad to leave. "The feeling" has disappeared. All I am now is nervous and sad.

Becky already has friends and knows her way around campus. I don't know anyone here. Has there ever been a time in my life where I was in a place where I knew no one? I don't think so. It's terrifying.

Just as we approach my building, Dad says, "Jo, I think it's time for us to get back on the road."

What did I think would happen? Did I think they would stay with me until I felt comfortable here?

"Becky, it was nice to meet you. If you ever need anything, please don't hesitate to ask," Mom says. They awkwardly hug. Dad shakes Becky's hand. With that, Becky heads up to our room.

Dad starts to say goodbye. Tears well up in my eyes. I knew I'd cry. This day has been so overwhelming. After my parents leave, I'll be all alone.

Mom and Dad take me into a hug. There's a big lump in my throat; I don't think I can do this without crying. Dad looks at me and says, "Everything is going to be okay. Just remember that your mom and I love you. We are so proud of you. We know you'll be great. Just be easy on yourself."

I give them a weak smile through my tears. I want my parents to know I'm okay, but Mom seems worried. She hugs me again and says, "I love you. We're only a phone call away."

"I love you both," I say. With that, they turn to leave. I walk to the door, and they turn back and wave with encouraging smiles.

CHAPTER 3

———

I make my way through the various groups of students and their parents with my head down so no one can see I've been crying. I finally reach the bathroom and, to my thankful surprise, no one is there but me. I quickly scrub my face with soap and splash some cold water on it. I use my hands to wipe the water out of my eyes and slowly open them. Of course I didn't get all the soap out and immediately feel the sting of soap in my left eye.

"Agh!" I panic, trying to wipe the soap out to no avail, and try to find something to pat my eye dry.

"You look like you could use some help. Here."

Opening my non-soapy eye, I see a petite Asian girl with a light purple bob haircut smiling and holding out some paper towels for me.

"I... I...I thought I was alone in here. Thanks, I really appreciate it."

"No problem! I was walking by and heard someone having trouble in here. Wow, saying that out loud sounds bad. People usually stay away from bathrooms if someone is *having trouble*."

Her emphasis on the last two words catch me totally off guard. I burst out laughing, and she joins in with relief, like she was a little embarrassed of her comment.

"I'm   Yu. I'm in 410."

"No way! I'm in 409. We must be neighbors. I'm Jo Prescott. I love your hair."

"Thanks! Last month, it was blue, and before that, it was pink. I thought purple would be a good way to start off college. It says, 'Hi, I'm cool and interesting.'"

"Totally!"

I blink my left eye a few times and finally open it.

"How's the eye doing?"

"Well, the stinging is gone, so that's a good sign. You're a lifesaver."

"No worries!"

I don't really know why, but I feel compelled to tell Ginger about my emotionally-filled morning. "I feel so embarrassed. I actually came in here to wash my face because I was just crying saying goodbye to my parents." I blush as I'm saying this out loud.

"Don't be embarrassed. It's normal. I try not to judge people. We're all entitled to our feelings. If I was closer with my parents, I probably would have cried saying goodbye."

I don't really know what to say. I can't imagine not being close with my parents.

Ginger must sense my pause. "I'm really close with my older sister. She's in Thailand this year, studying abroad. I miss her like crazy. I'm going to visit her over winter break, so I'll see her soon enough and then I can eat as much pad thai, tom yum goong, and curry as I want!" Ginger has a wistful smile on her face, as if she's already picturing what her trip to Thailand with her sister will be like.

"Wow, that's awesome. I've never actually had Thai food bef—" I cut off as I see Ginger's face change from a smile to one of shock. Her jaw is basically on the floor.

"You've never had Thai food before? How is this possible? You're missing out on one of the most delicious cultures on the planet," she says, unable to fathom my very boring palate.

"My parents aren't very adventurous when it comes to food. The only takeout we get is pizza on Fridays or, if they're feeling crazy, chicken parm subs from the same place. When I go to the diner with my friends, I get banana chocolate chip pancakes." I say, proud of my order. Yum, I already miss those pancakes...

"You have no idea what you're missing. Have you ever had sushi? Or dim sum? Or Indian food? Korean BBQ?"

"Dim sum? I've never even heard those words before." I shake my head, a little embarrassed that I'm not very adventurous with my food choices.

"Dim sum is a style of Chinese cuisine. Cantonese, if we're being particular. It's hard to explain what dim sum is; it's better to just experience it. But damn, Jo. I'm shocked you haven't even had Thai food! Where did you say you grew up?"

"In a small town outside of New York City."

This throws her for another loop.

"How could you not have tried any of this food? New York City is the epicenter for all things food and culture."

I think she notices I'm a little embarrassed, and she quickly says, "It's okay, Jo. It just means we have a lot of work to do!" A mischievous smile spreads across her face.

I can't help but giggle at her. "Oh, God, what does that mean?"

"We are going to have to educate you on food. We'll call it your fooducation! I don't know how great the options will be downtown, we are in the middle of Pennsylvania, but we'll make do." It seems like Ginger is deep in thought, probably strategically planning my "fooducation."

This actually sounds fun. I feel like Jo Prescott for the first time all day. "Well, let's start easy! You're talking to a girl who has eaten frozen waffles for breakfast every day of her life for the last ten years. I'm a creature of habit."

"Okay, I'm thinking Thai food first."

"I trust you."

As Ginger and I are walking out of the bathroom and back toward our rooms, she says, "You know, I actually live in New Jersey, not far from Manhattan. Maybe over Thanksgiving break, we can do a *real* fooducation. K-town, here we come!"

"Sounds fun!" I can't help but smile. Although I met her unconventionally, Ginger is really cool and down to earth. She seems like someone I can really be friends with.

"Crap, I'm late to Facetime my sister. Let me get your number!" Ginger says enthusiastically.

We exchange numbers and head our separate ways.

* * *

I'm standing in front of my room, fighting my anxiety. It's time to face Becky.

I open my door. It takes my brain a moment to register exactly what I'm looking at. But when I finally understand what I'm seeing, I gasp.

Becky is straddling someone and making out with them. Aggressive may not be a strong enough word to describe Becky right now.

Becky must have heard me gasp because she turns around and says, "Hey, Jo!" with a smile on her face. As she's turning back to the person underneath her, I swear I catch her rolling her eyes.

Is this a normal thing for her? I've only made out with two boys in my life and both were very private experiences. I've never kissed someone in front of anyone. I'd be humiliated!

My first kiss was with a boy from a local summer camp after my freshman year of high school. We were both camp counselors teaching tennis to little kids. One particular hot and humid day after camp, we went back to his house to swim in his pool. His parents weren't home. I had a little crush on him, and I guess he must have had one on me, too, because before I knew it, he was kissing me in the pool.

The second kiss was senior year with my prom date. We had been friends throughout high school and went to prom as friends—or so I thought. After prom, we went to the Jersey Shore for senior weekend. We had been drinking on his motel room's balcony, just talking, and I think the alcohol and the fact that this was our last hurrah got us in a certain mood. We made out for about twenty minutes before deciding we better leave it as a one-time thing.

"I'm so sorry for...interrupting. Should I come back?" I manage to get out.

Becky was about to respond when I see the guy she was making out with. I immediately recognize the hazel eyes from earlier that day. It's Hot Boy Matt from the welcome desk. And I'm completely mortified.

The recognition is on Matt's face as well and to my surprise, he turns red. "Uh, I'd better go." He gently moves Becky off him and, with his head down, walks past me out the door.

"That was weird!" Becky says, as chipper as ever.

I can tell Becky seems to think it's unusual that Matt got up and left, but is not in the slightest bit concerned I walked in on them.

"Yeah...sorry about that. My parents left and I wanted to finish unpacking."

"It's okay. I was just having a little fun."

"So, you and him...?"

"He was walking up and down the hallway making sure everyone was settling in all right. He knocked on our door. I think it's because I'm in the Lululemon pants that accentuate my butt. I thought he was hot, so I asked if he wanted to come in and he did. Seemed like he was waiting around for something, and I was getting bored, so I thought, why not spice things up?"

I can't help it—I look at her butt. Of course, she's right. Those Lululemon pants *do* accentuate her assets. I'm not surprised. I should have known Hot Boy Matt was into tall, gorgeous model types. Is this what I have to look forward to all year? Being in Becky's shadow as she brings boys back to our room?

I'm at a loss for words so I busy myself by hanging up pictures on my wall.

Not sure what else to say, I ask, "What's you major?" That's a normal thing to ask other college students, right?

"I'm pre-law. I want to become a lawyer. That's actually one of the reasons I did summer semester—to get ahead on classes."

"That was smart." I reply, not sure what else to say.

"Yeah, but a little voice in my head said, 'Becky, this is the time to enjoy yourself and let loose.' So I did! Now it's time to actually buckle down and study. Okay, maybe just *one* more semester of fun!"

"Wow, pre-law, that's awesome." I slowly sit on my bed, letting my thoughts wander.

Becky wants to be a lawyer? She seems like a wild child who wants to have fun and party, not someone who's going to go to four years of undergrad and then another three years of law school.

Suddenly, it dawns on me. Becky is the most confident person I have ever met. She made out with a random guy who walked into our room. I would never do something like that! What if the guy pushed me away and said he wasn't interested or that I had bad breath? She wants to be a lawyer; that's a big undertaking, but she seems to have the conviction. I'm impressed. This girl is ahead of me in every aspect—boys, school, fun. It reminds me of all the things I don't have going on in my life.

A few minutes go by, but Becky doesn't ask about my major and I don't volunteer the information. I guess she doesn't really care.

Since this conversation seems to have ended, I lie on my bed, looking at the ceiling tiles. I put my headphones in and go back to my Alt Punk playlist on Spotify. As Bon Iver sings "Skinny Love" in my ear, I can't help but think that my insecurities about Becky seem to be coming true.

CHAPTER 4

———

I must have nodded off because a knock at our door wakes me up. I'm disoriented until I see Becky stride across the room to let in our visitors. Suddenly, I'm rubbing my eyes, trying to wake myself up. Who could be here? I literally have drool dried onto my chin. How embarrassing.

Two girls stand at our door. One is a tall, thin redhead with big boobs and a perfect nose, wearing tight low-cut shorts and a crop top. Her hair reminds me of Ariel from *The Little Mermaid* with its bright, unnatural red. I have to admit, it looks great on her. The other girl is shorter than her friend but still taller than I am, with dark, wild, curly hair, and a short floral dress.

"What's up, bitches!" Becky says in a high-pitched voice.

I guess these are Becky's friends she met over the summer.

Becky turns to my direction and says to them, "Abby, Ellie, this is my roommate, Jo!"

The girls make their way into the room and, to my shock, Abby plops herself right down at the edge of my bed and starts scrolling through Instagram on her phone. It's a little too familiar for me. I mean, it's my bed and I barely know her. Should I tell her to please move? Before I can make up my mind, my attention moves to Ellie when she says my name.

"Hey, Jo, it's nice to meet you. I'm Ellie," says the brunette with a sweet smile on her face. "When did you move in?"

"I moved in this morning. My parents just left a few hours ago. Do you live on this floor?"

"Abby and I actually met Becky over the summer. We all did summer semester and lived in the same building. Abby and I are roommates in Montgomery on the north part of campus."

"Damn, you're so lucky! I actually applied for Montgomery but was placed here."

Without looking up from her phone, Abby chimes in, "Ugh, why would you want to live in Montgomery? Your dorms are so much nicer here, and you're closer to town. Easy access to all the parties."

I can already tell I don't like Abby's vibe. I barely know her and she seems...I'm not quite sure, but annoyed with me?

"I guess I was just looking for the true freshman experience."

Ellie jumps in, "I don't know if the 'true freshman experience' is a good thing or a bad thing. This morning, we woke up to the smell of weed wafting into our room, and there was puke waiting for us in the bathroom sink." She chuckles, and I can tell she's trying to make me feel more at ease.

I think I like Ellie, but why is she hanging out with Abby?

"Anyway," says Abby, clearly bored with our conversation. "Are we going out tonight or *what*?" She ends her sentence with a dramatic eye roll. Is it too soon to dub this as a "classic" Abby move?

Despite myself, I ask, "Where are you all going?"

Becky gives me a sly look. "You mean, where are *we* going."

Oh, God. This cannot be happening. There is nothing less appealing to me right now than going out with Abby.

I start to shake my head. "I don't think—"

Becky cuts me off. "Come on, Jo! It's your first night at college. It's time to have fun." Either I'm imagining things, or it sounds like Becky has an edge to her voice.

Not wanting to be rude, I say, "Thank you for inviting me."

Becky arches her eyebrow at me as if to say, *are you really going to turn me down?*

I quickly say, "Really! That was so nice. I was hoping to stay in tonight and get ready for classes tomorrow." I tell them the partial truth. The other reason I don't want to go out is because I don't really want to go out in a new place with people I just met... I guess most college freshmen probably don't share this same view.

Abby rolls her eyes and says, "Figures."

I try my best to keep my jaw from hitting the floor. Did she really just say that? But what happens next stuns me even more.

Becky stifles a laugh.

The blood rushes to my face, and my hands start to prickle, sweat forming immediately. A part of me feels...I don't know, lame? Why didn't I just say I would go? Stupid, stupid Jo.

The other part of me is telling the first part, *stop that!* I shouldn't let Abby and Becky make me feel bad about not wanting to go out. *Stand your ground, Jo!*

"It's okay, Jo! I didn't want to go out much when I first got here over the summer either," Ellie says, throwing me a metaphorical life preserver. She's looking at me like I'm an injured animal.

I nod at her to reassure her that I'm okay. I can't figure Ellie out. It doesn't seem like she fits in with these two.

"Yeah, Jo, you can come out with us another time." Becky waves her hand in the air, dismissing me. She turns to Abby and says, "So, what should I wear tonight?"

I've had enough of Becky and Abby for one evening. I grab my bag and say, "I'm going for a walk. See you later."

Becky and Abby don't even acknowledge me. Ellie gives me a weak smile like she's apologizing for the other two. I hope to God that by the time I get back, they're nowhere to be seen.

As I leave my room and close the door behind me, I hear Abby say loudly, "Your roommate is a loser."

I feel a twinge of annoyance. That jerk. I couldn't care less what she thinks of me, but I can't help myself, so I stay for another minute to listen in on their conversation from the other side of the door.

"Ellie was the same way when we met her! And look at her now. Right, Ell?" Becky replies. I hear her laughing through the wall.

I listen intently, waiting for Ellie's response, but it never comes.

I quietly back away from the door, and, taking my time, make my way outside. My thoughts drift.

Becky hangs out with people like Abby...Becky *is* people like Abby. No, maybe I'm being too harsh? Maybe I just caught Becky on a weird day? Maybe I'm blowing this out of proportion. Despite the feeling in my gut, I decide to give Becky the benefit of the doubt. I have to live with her for the next nine months.

At least I met Ginger. *Ginger!*

I get my phone out and text her.

You want to order takeout and hang out later?

Seconds later, I get a reply.

Only if it's Thai food. She adds an emoji with its tongue sticking out.

I smile at myself and shake my head. I guess I'm trying Thai food for the first time tonight.

Cool, meet at my room in an hour?

Get ready to have your taste buds explode.

That sounds violent. I try my best at a joke.

She sends me back the rolling-eye emoji and the laughing emoji. My joke landed!

I put my phone away and continue on my walk through campus.

* * *

I'm back at my room an hour later and pause in front of my door before saying a silent prayer to the universe, hoping Becky and her friends won't be there. I take a deep breath and push on the door. It's locked! That's a good sign. With a big smile across my face, I unlock my door.

My smile fades quickly. My room is a mess. Half-full red solo cups, empty bottles of Gatorade, and makeup are littered all over the desks and the pungent smell of vodka fills the air. I step over the threshold, and my foot sticks to the floor. Looking down, I see a puddle of something. Probably someone's spilled drink. Gross.

I cross the room and yank open the window as fast as I can. This room desperately needs fresh air. Becky and her friends were either too drunk to care about cleaning up or just didn't give a shit. My vote is on the latter.

I grab a garbage bag from my closet and start to throw out the garbage on our desks when I hear a knock at the door.

"Come in!"

"Whoa. What happened in here? It reeks." Ginger uses her fingers to pinch her nose.

"My roommate happened."

"Here, let me help." Ginger disappears for a few moments and reappears with a wad of paper towels in her hand. She kneels and uses the paper towels to soak up the mystery puddle.

"Thanks." I give Ginger a small smile.

We work in silence for a few minutes. Then Ginger says, "So, what's up with your roommate? Is she like a crazy person or something?" The way she says it makes me laugh.

"She's definitely something. She and her friends were planning to go out. I guess the pre-game happened here. Maybe this is their way of sticking it to me because I didn't want to go out with them."

"Oooh, tell me more."

"One of her friends called me a loser."

"Oh, no, she didn't."

Saying it out loud makes it seem even more ridiculous. "It's actually kind of funny. Girls making fun of other girls because they don't want to go out. Isn't that judgment supposed to end when you get to college?"

"Damn. That shit makes me so angry. I can't stand girls like that."

"Right?" I instantly feel closer with Ginger.

We finish cleaning up the room, and to my relief, the smell has somewhat disappeared.

"So, what should we order for dinner?" I say, playing dumb.

"Don't even, Jo! We agreed on Thai food. I'll order. I can't be friends with someone who has never tried pad see eew or massaman curry."

"I don't know what any of those words mean, but hey, you did just clean mystery goo off the floor. I owe you one. Dinner's on me."

"Oh, I thought you paying was always the plan."

This girl's a character. I can get used to her.

* * *

An hour and seventy dollars worth of Thai food later, Ginger and I are both stuffed. Ginger is lying on Becky's bed, I'm on mine, and we have *The Office* playing on the laptop on my desk chair in the middle of the room.

"I have to say, Thai food is pretty good. The drunken noodles were my favorite." I sit up and reach for the plastic takeout container to finish it off.

"Drunken noodles are the most Americanized dish we got tonight! What about the curries?"

"Give me a break, I'm new to this! I'm expanding my palate. You should be happy with that."

"I guess you're right. Next time, Indian food!"

I yawn and lay back down on my bed.

"You can't be tired already. It's only ten!"

"I've never been good at staying up late. I always fall asleep during movies and stuff." I think my eyes are closed. I'm getting sleepy.

I hear Ginger walking around the room but I'm too tired to open my eyes to see what she's doing.

"Night, Jo." The door closes quietly behind her.

* * *

A loud crashing noise startles me awake. I turn the light on to see what's happening, adrenaline pumping through my veins.

"Oops, sorry, Jo," says what appears to be a very drunk Becky. She's lying on the floor with pens and pencils scattered all around her. She must have knocked them over on her way in.

"Oh, God, I think I'm going to be sick." I don't even have time to look away as Becky pukes all over our floor.

You've got to be kidding me.

My annoyances turns to panic. I'm one of those people who can't deal with vomit. The smell alone makes me queasy.

"Becky!"

No response.

I take a deep breath to calm myself down and walk over to where Becky lies on the floor.

She's asleep. I shake her shoulders, but all I hear is soft snoring.

DAY 2

CHAPTER 5

Beep...beep...beep...beep...

I pull my hand out from under the covers and snooze my phone alarm. I groan loudly into my pillow. How can it be 6:30 already?

I try to sleep for another fifteen minutes but Becky's snoring is so damn loud. Opening my eyes, I find she's no longer sprawled out on our bedroom floor. She must have gotten up at some point and realized the cold, hard cement floor isn't the most comfortable place to sleep. Who would have thought?

Maybe I'd be better rested if I hadn't been up until two in the morning cleaning Becky's vomit off the floor. Ugh. Thinking about it makes my stomach turn. Is this what I have to look forward to the rest of the year?

Shake it off, Jo! Time to start the day.

I throw my legs over the side of my bed and grab my shower caddy as I head out the door. It's super quiet in the hallway and, to my relief, there is no one else in the communal bathrooms.

The shower stalls look exactly like the bathroom stalls from the outside: smooth gray concrete that reaches from the floor to the ceiling. Both look like they were built sometime in the 1960s, and that's being generous. The only difference is, on the inside, there's a shower head and bench as opposed to a toilet. Why there is a bench in the shower, I have no idea. How many butts have sat on that thing?

Not gonna lie, this is so weird. I'm about to shower in a bathroom that doesn't even have doors that lead to the hallway, just open archways. Nothing is stopping a random guy—or a random anyone—from just walking in.

Deep breaths. I stare at the shower stall in front of me. Well, here goes nothing.

I choose the shower stall farthest to the left so I only have one other shower next to me. I try pulling the door open, but it doesn't budge. I plant my feet more firmly on the floor, use one hand to make sure my towel is secure around my body, and use my other hand to tug as hard as I can to get the door open. The door finally opens but I fall backward right onto my shower caddy. Ow. Ew. I quickly scramble to my feet so I'm not on the bathroom floor much longer.

I close myself into the shower stall and lock the door as fast as I can. Being naked in a communal bathroom is enough to make me paranoid. I turn the knob for the water, and I hear the loud whooshing of it running through the rickety pipes. Water spits out in all different directions—in my eyes, in my mouth, and to the sides of the shower. Basically, everywhere except where I want it to go. I miss my shower at home. At least the water's warm.

* * *

In forty-five minutes, I'm dressed and ready to leave for my first day of classes—dry hair, minty fresh breath, and my fully packed backpack. I have my favorite white jean shorts, same as yesterday, and a peach tank top. I put my hair in a neat ballerina bun on top of my head. I'm surprisingly happy with what I see in the mirror.

I check my phone for the time. 7:30 a.m.

My first class is at eight, and it's across campus. I'm not really familiar with how to get there, so I figure I'll give myself lots of time, just in case.

There's something about the first day of school that gives me a surge of excitement. Today marks a new chapter, a fresh start. Plus, going to class means getting out of my room, and far, far away from Becky.

It's chilly out for an August morning. I regret not bringing a sweater with me. Do I run upstairs to get it? No, I don't want to be late for class.

Huge, majestic trees with bright green leaves line the sidewalks on campus. The sun is shining and I can't help but bask in it. It's really quiet on campus. Eerily quiet for a campus that has forty thousand students.

A brick building with the name *TWIG* written across the front comes into view; I made it to my first class. Nerves wash over me. My hands become clammy and my heart beats faster.

I push through the large wooden doors, and I'm immediately hit with a musty stale smell, like old books. The classrooms are old, with chalkboards on the walls and outdated desks.

7:45 a.m.

Fifteen minutes early! *Note to self: you don't need half an hour to walk to class.*

With nothing else to do, I take a seat in the front of the classroom. There's not a soul here, not even the professor. *Damn, Jo, you gave yourself way too much time!* There are only about forty desks; this must be one of my smallest classes. Most classes as a freshman at PSC are in the hundreds.

Over the next several minutes, the class starts to fill up, and a few girls sit to the left of me. The professor finally arrives, and it seems like class is about to start. I grab my glasses from my bag so I can see the board better and, as I turn to my right, I see none other than Hot Guy Matt walk through the door. Holy shit.

He looks a little out of breath, like he ran here. He's in sweatpants and a T-shirt with his sweatshirt slung over his shoulder. He seems out of sorts, but who am I kidding, he's still cute. *Dammit, Matt, why do you have to be so cute?*

He notices me and a smile stretches across his face, causing flutters in my stomach and tingles all the way down my spine. Is he looking at me?

"Hey, 409!" Without a drop of hesitation, he plops down in the seat next to me. *409...he remembers me!*

"Hey, yep, that's me...but you can call me Jo."

"Jo...I like it! It's nice to officially meet you. I'm Matt."

"I remember." *Oh, God, did I just say that out loud?* How embarrassing. Trying to change the direction of the conversation, I ask, "You're a freshman?" My curiosity gets the better of me. He's part of the Welcome Committee—he can't be a freshman.

"Yeah, I am. I was here for summer semester actually. I met some of the Welcome Crew people, and they asked if I could lend a hand moving students in, so I figured, why not? Plus, I got to move in a week early, which was nice. The calm before the storm."

"It was wild yesterday! I've never seen so many people in my whole life, and I live near the city."

"Which city?" He looks at me like he's sincerely interested in my answer.

"The best city there is—New York." I'm proud of where I come from.

"No way! We probably don't live too far apart. I'm in Jersey, down the shore."

I can't help but smile. It feels good to talk to someone about home. "I grew up going to the Jersey Shore during the summer as a kid." I blush before adding, "I guess a lot of people do from our area."

"Maybe we've crossed paths before." He gives me a shy smile, and my heart skips a beat. Before I have a chance to respond, the professor starts class. I tear my eyes away from him and try my best to listen to the lecture to no avail. My mind is on Matt and our common threads.

* * *

My first college class ends without incident, thank God. We get our syllabus for the semester, and I'm already planning out my first assignment in my head.

I'm ready to go so I turn to say something to Matt. What should I even say to him? *Bye? What class do you have next?*

I'm about to ask Matt a very casual version of "Where ya headed now?" when I catch him staring at me. Oh, God, was I muttering to myself out loud or something? Do I have something in my teeth? Do I have a stain on my shirt? I begin to look down at my clothes and try to discreetly smell my armpit.

Finally, I say, "What are you looking at?"

Completely avoiding my question, Matt says, "Do you want to grab some coffee?"

Electricity courses through my veins. I nod in agreement. My next class isn't for another hour.

We make our way outside and the sun is shining brightly. Out of habit, I stop and tilt my head up to the sun with my eyes closed and take a deep inhale. I momentarily forget where I am and who I'm with. A few seconds later, I open my eyes and feel more calm than I have in the past twenty-four hours.

Matt is looking at me like he's trying to figure me out. His look of bewilderment makes me laugh. I should be embarrassed, but I'm not for some reason.

"I love the sun," I say to him simply and smile.

He smiles in return, probably unsure what to say to this weirdo.

A few minutes later, we make it to the north campus coffee shop. When we get to the front of the line, I greet the student behind the counter. "Hi, can I get...hmm, an iced tea with lemon?"

The girl smiles and turns to make my drink.

"What, no coffee? A girl from New York and she doesn't drink coffee?" Matt says behind me, his tone teasing.

"Like I haven't heard that before! I grew up in a tea household. I've tried coffee a few times and just never got into it. It's so bitter!" I scrunch up my face just thinking about it.

I pay for my tea and Matt orders black coffee.

"Very English of you. I, on the other hand, started drinking coffee at the young age of five."

"Wow, your family started you young, huh?"

Matt starts laughing. "My grandma used to give me coffee as a kid; just a little though. She was old-school Italian. Since then, I've always loved the taste of coffee. Plus, it reminds me of my Nan." His eyes get wistful, and he hesitates before continuing, "She passed away last year. I miss her every day."

Poor Matt. "I'm so sorry. She sounds like a fun lady." I smile, trying to cheer him up.

"She was hilarious. She would say things at the dinner table that would make you spit out your food."

We take our drinks and find a table outside. It's a beautiful day out. Sunny with a light breeze. It definitely feels slightly cooler here than back home. I like it.

"So do you come from a big Italian family?" I say, curious to learn more about him.

"Is it that obvious? I'm the oldest in my family. I have four younger sisters."

"Wow." I can't hide my shock. "You must have had a hectic house growing up." I put my hand under my chin and lean my elbow on the table.

"Hectic is too small of a word for what my house is like. I wouldn't have it any other way. My next oldest sister is four years younger than me, and then my sisters are each two years apart in age. They fight over everything—clothes, phones, food, you name it. What about you?"

"I have two brothers. One older, one younger. There were a lot of video games in my house growing up. I wasn't interested in those, so my brothers and I never really fought. I miss them."

Matt puts his hand over mine, I assume in a comforting gesture, but my face immediately heats up. I stare at his beautiful face. He's staring right back.

My phone beeps, breaking our trance.

Reluctantly, I pull my hand from underneath his and check my phone. There's a group text from my parents that says, *Good luck on your first day!* I smile to myself. My eye catches the time. Holy shit!

"I'm going to be late to my next class! I gotta go. I'll see you around, Matt!"

He has a pout on his face since I'm leaving so abruptly, and I can't help but be giddy about it.

DAY 30

CHAPTER 6

"All right, everyone, since it's Homecoming weekend, I'm letting you out twenty minutes early. I know I'm the best, you're welcome!"

There's collective cheering among our class. It's no surprise that Matt's cheering the loudest. He's so cute.

The last few weeks have been such a blur. Full of class, studying, late night takeout with Ginger, post-class coffee with Matt, and avoiding Becky whenever possible.

"Pretty sweet that he let us out early, I'm beat. Who knew college would so exhausting? And I sleep until eleven most days!" Matt's smiling, waiting for me to comment.

"Yeah, even on days you're supposed to be in this class!" I stick my tongue out so he knows I'm just teasing.

"Hey! I'll have you know I've only accidentally slept through this class twice."

"Sure. And the other days, you're just ten minutes late."

"Ouch, I'm hurt, Jo." Matt feigns putting his hand over his heart.

"Oh, please!" I roll my eyes.

We fall into step with each other as we walk to our coffee shop for our normal post-class routine. Since it's cooler out today, I decide to order a hot earl grey tea with cream and sugar and wait while Matt orders his black coffee.

"So, what are you up to this weekend?" Matt asks.

"Hmmm, not sure. Probably sleeping in and binging something on Netflix. I usually stay in on weekends."

Matt suddenly looks anything but calm. He's tapping his fingers on the counter, waiting for his coffee. "Maybe we should change that."

I think my breathing stops altogether for a few seconds. What is he asking me? To hang out? To go out?

"Jo?"

"Sorry, what did you say?"

"I said maybe we should change that. You should come out with me tonight. Someone is throwing a surprise birthday party for one of my friends."

"I don't know..." I'm so nervous! Can I get through a whole night with Matt without making a complete fool of myself?

"Come on, Jo! It'll be fun! I'll stick by your side all night, scout's honor." He pulls up his hand and salutes me.

I can't say no to that face. I giggle. "Okay, I'll think about it!" I grab my tea and walk to find our normal table, not waiting for him to catch up. I look over my shoulder and watch him clumsily grab his coffee and walk after me.

* * *

All day, I can't help but think about Matt's invitation. I've been wrestling with my inner dialog all day. Do I stay in or do I go out with Matt? What if we go out and he doesn't like me anymore? Or thinks I'm boring?

My nerves get the best of me. I can't go.

I send Matt a quick text:

Hey Matt! Can't make it tonight. Tell your friend I say Happy Birthday! See you Monday. :)

I hit send and immediately feel regret. Maybe even sadness?

Trying to distract myself, I go find Ginger.

"Thank God you're here. I'm starving! What do you want for dinner?" For someone who is so tiny, Ginger eats a lot. It's one of my favorite things about her.

"Chipotle?" I say, with hope in my voice. It's one of my favorites, but I know this is going to be a hard sell to Ginger.

Ginger rolls her eyes. "Come on. Chipotle is so mainstream!"

"Who cares if it's mainstream? Their chicken bowl is delicious. It's good for the soul. Don't pretend you don't like it. Everyone likes Chipotle. It's like the America's Sweetheart of fast food." I know Ginger likes Chipotle; Ginger knows she likes Chipotle. Now she just has to admit it out loud.

Ginger crosses her arms over her chest, like she's debating her options, but I can tell her defenses are down. I'm about to win! Chicken bowl, medium salsa, spicy corn, here I come!

"I guess I can just go without you?" I flash my best puppy dog eyes at her. I know she can't say no to them.

"Fine! Okay, I'll admit it. Chipotle is fine... for a chain restaurant."

I roll my eyes. "Let's go."

Ginger closes the door behind her, and I hear her whisper to herself excitedly, "I'm going to get extra guac."

"This line. Why is it always a hundred people long?" Ginger exclaims.

I can't argue with her on that. The only downside to Chipotle is its popularity, causing long lines out the door. Even though the staff works fast, it still takes about twenty-five minutes just to get to the front of the line. At least now we're inside, where I can smell the spices and seasoned grilled meats. It's so close I can almost taste it. Literally.

But I can't admit to Ginger that waiting in line sucks, so I say, "My brother once told me the best places to eat have the longest lines. We already know Chipotle is the best Mexican food ever." I don't really think that—I'm no fool, but I can't help but push Ginger's buttons.

Ginger's eyes narrow. "Don't start with me. I'm hangry. Why insult me with such words?" She starts counting the people ahead of us in line.

My phone vibrates, and I feel a panic wash over me. I know who it is before I even look at my phone. Matt. He responded.

:(

Underneath his text, I see the all too well-known iPhone ellipses. He's typing. The anticipation is killing me.

Is there anything I can say to convince you to come out?

"Who's texting you?" asks Ginger.

Of course! I need advice. I quickly fill Ginger in on the Matt situation and his invitation for tonight.

"Why don't you want to go?"

"I'm nervous! He's really hot, and I don't know how to play it cool. We have fun when go for coffee. That seems...safe? Going out with him just seems like another level."

"Just go! What's the worst that can happen? You have a bad time? You and Coffee Boy don't hit it off? You need to be more open to new opportunities! That's what college is about."

"Uh huh, coming from the girl who fought tooth and nail when I suggested Chipotle for dinner."

"That's different. I'm encouraging you to do things outside of your comfort zone!"

"I don't know..."

Ginger puts her hands on my shoulders. "As your friend, I'm demanding you go out. Live a little!"

I think about Ginger's words. I *should* go for it. "You're right—"

Ginger holds up her finger to me. "White rice, double chicken, spicy salsa, veggies, and extra guac on the side... with chips."

"For someone who hates Chipotle, you really have your order down to a science."

"Just because Chipotle isn't my favorite place doesn't mean I don't know my way around a burrito bowl."

While Ginger is busy arguing with the Chipotle employees that they didn't give her enough chicken, I quickly shoot a text to Matt.

Change of plans, I'm in!

* * *

"What am I going to wear tonight?" I say out loud in an exasperated sigh even though no one's around to answer my question.

I'm in my room, pacing the small space. I'm glad Becky isn't here. I need some calm before my date, and I can't relax when I see her. All I can think of when she's around is the memory of her vomiting on our floor. At least our room doesn't smell anymore. It only took three weeks of sleeping with the window open every night in the forty-degree weather for it to air out.

I start taking out everything I own and lay it on my bed. What a complete disaster.

Suddenly, it dawns on me. I'll wear my red velvet tank and my black skinny jeans. It's cute and flirty...flirty? Who am I?

I begin rifling through all the clothes on my bed. Not here. Where is that shirt? I check under my bed and in my drawers. It's my favorite one...I don't even think I've worn it since I've been here.

I'm in the middle of going through the bins under my bed when Becky walks in.

She nods in my direction. We haven't really spoken much since the incident. Still, I can't help but think about it. It's instant, as soon as I see her.

As much as it pains me to speak to her, I know I have to. "Hey, Becky, have you seen my red velvet tank? I can't find it anywhere."

Becky is changing her clothes so quickly I almost don't realize she's doing it.

Touching up her makeup, she says, "Hmm, nope. Haven't seen it."

Call it crazy intuition, but I don't believe her.

"Are you sure? It's not in your closet or in one of your drawers?"

She closes her closet semi-aggressively and looks me square in the face. "No, I haven't seen it. What are you insinuating?"

I'm too stunned to even answer. Only guilty people are this defensive.

Not waiting for my answer, she says, "I'm leaving."

"Where are you going?" I don't even know why I asked; it doesn't matter.

"It's Friday night, I'm going out."

"Say hi to Ellie and Abby for me!" I call to her as she storms out of our room. Sarcasm isn't a good look on me, but I can't help it. I know she's lying about my shirt. I can feel it in my gut.

I give myself a few minutes just to make sure Becky's not coming back. Then I go through her stuff like a madwoman— the closet, drawers, everything.

Crazy. I'm crazy. I'm having a moment of clarity...*Don't stoop to her level. This is a violation of privacy.*

As I'm hanging up the last of her clothes, I see it. My favorite red velvet shirt, crumpled in a ball, at the bottom of her laundry basket...with a huge stain across the front.

Dammit, Becky.

CHAPTER 7

———

How could she? Why would she?

Those two questions repeat in my head as I rush around trying to find something else to wear for the night. Shirts, pants, and dresses are no longer just on my bed but strewn around my room. I better put it all away before Becky gets back—I don't want any more of my stuff to go missing.

I finally settle on my light pink wrap sweater. It looks like something a ballerina would wear, with my black skinny jeans and knee-high black riding boots. I'm not really sure what "going out" clothes are because I've never really gone out. I hope this is okay.

This place is a disaster. I start grabbing everything I can and shoving it under my bed when I hear a knock at the door.

Oh my God, he's here! I finish stuffing the last dress under my bed and take a quick glance in the mirror. It's as good as it's gonna get tonight.

"Come in!" I shout.

The door slowly pushes open, and Matt peeks his head around hesitantly. Even though he has a goofy look on his face, like he's a spy running a covert mission, my heart still skips a beat. When he sees me, his eyes widen in fake surprise.

I can't help but giggle.

"Hey, 409! Didn't know I'd be seeing you here," Matt jokes.

When Matt says things like this, I can't help but think, *hot guys can be corny?* Usually, hot guys take themselves too seriously...right? Not this one. He seems too good to be true.

"You're ridiculous." I roll my eyes, but when he jokes around with me like this, it feels like there are thousands of butterflies in my stomach having a party. I can't complain. I love the butterflies, and I like that Matt gives them to me.

"You ready?" Matt's smile is stretching across his whole face.

"Hmm, I guess that depends." I smile as wide as I can too. Why is smiling the best?

"On?"

"If you're ready! You know there's a lot of pressure on you. I haven't gone out since I've been at PSC. I'm expecting my mind to be blown."

"Oh. It'll be blown. I have some tricks up my sleeve." He yanks at his sleeve.

"Okay, okay! Let's get this show on the road then!" My face hurts from smiling so hard.

I push him playfully out of the room and lock the door behind us.

"Geez, someone is impatient...or is it excited? For the best night ever?"

Instead of answering him, I start laughing and run down the hallway so he has to catch me.

* * *

"Okay, so. Are you ready for the first stop of the night? I don't want to brag, but it's pretty cool. Some would say, the best first stop of any night." Somehow, Matt says this without sounding remotely cocky. How does he do that?

I'm under his spell. "I'll be the judge of that!" I like this fun banter. He brings out this goofy side of me. "So, where is this magical first stop?"

"Oh, no. I'm not telling you. It's a surprise."

I'm going for it. I look at Matt and give him my very best puppy dog eyes and pouty lip.

Matt puts his hand up to block my face. "That's not going to work on me. I can be immune to cute girl charm when I try hard enough."

"Aww, man, the puppy dog eyes always work on Ginger!" My mind is racing a million miles a minute. Did he just call me cute? His words temporarily disarm my attempt to get information out of him when our eyes meet. What he does next stuns me into silence.

Matt reaches down and takes my hand in his. He takes his time interlacing our fingers and giving them a gentle squeeze when they're in place. Electricity courses through my veins. My first thought is that his hands are *huge*. My immediate second thought is *holy shit*. He's holding my hand. *We're* holding hands.

He starts pulling me along. "Come on, slowpoke. If we move any slower, we'll miss the surprise part of the surprise party." There's a hint of teasing in his voice, but it's also a lot softer now, like maybe he doesn't want to rush this part of the night.

I'm not really sure what to say or do, so I do the oldest thing in the book: blush and tuck a pretend stray hair behind my ear. That's what girls do, right? When they're trying to be cute?

"We're almost there," he says.

I'm so distracted by our hand holding I almost forgot about the "first stop" of the night. The anticipation starts to rise in my chest. I've never actually been to this part of campus. I have no clue where he's taking me.

We round a corner and a dome comes into view. I look over at Matt, whose eyes light up. They are quite literally lit by the glowing dome.

"Come on!" He pulls my hand, and we pick up our pace as we head toward the building.

We stop right in front of the door. "What is it?" I ask.

"Let's go in and find out." He gives me a mischievous smile and pushes the door open.

"Is this allowed?" I ask anxiously.

All I get in response is a chuckle.

What I see when we walk through the door is mesmerizing. It looks like a jungle—green plants and vibrant colored flowers in every single direction. Is it a greenhouse? It looks too lush and alive to be just a simple greenhouse. It's not just rows of plants on tables, it's different types of trees all around us, flowers—tons of different colored flowers—hanging from the ceiling. It feels more like the rainforest.

"Wow, it's beautiful." I stroll down one walkway lined with orange and yellow exotic-looking flowers. They're tall enough that I can easily touch them, but I don't. Instead, I opt to smell them. They smell sweet and warm, like summer.

"Yeah, it's pretty great. It's run and maintained by the botany department. My roommate is a horticultural science major. He told me about this place. It's usually open to the public, but on Friday nights they're closed."

"Should we be here right now? Are we going to get in trouble?" I look over my shoulder at the door to check that no one has caught us.

"We won't get caught. So...what do you think? Good surprise?"

I take a step toward Matt so I can see his face. "Great surprise."

Matt's staring into my eyes. My heart begins racing, and my breath quickens. All the teasing and joking from earlier in the night has vanished. It's replaced with heat, tension... and anticipation.

Matt gently puts his hands on my waist and pauses momentarily, waiting to see my reaction. I look up at him under my lashes and slowly nod. He lifts his hand and brushes my cheek before placing it on the back of my head. My cheek tingles in the places he touched.

So slowly it's almost torturous, Matt pulls me closer to him and ducks his head so his lips can meet mine.

The moment they do, I feel a passion and a yearning I've never felt before. Every one of my senses feels alive. Our lips move in sync, and my hands are all over him. Moving up his chest, feeling the muscles in his arms, and pulling him closer to me, even though there isn't any room between us.

I could kiss him for hours. Which is why, when he gently pulls away, I let out a sound between a sigh and a groan.

Matt chuckles at my reaction and then whispers in my ear, "We're going to be late for the party, Jo."

"Who cares?" I pull him toward me again and start to kiss him slowly and knot my fingers through his hair.

Between kisses, Matt says, "Okay, just a few more minutes." I smile to myself as he kisses down my neck. Victory!

* * *

We're sitting on a bench in the garden, with my head on Matt's shoulder and our hands intertwined. My head is still reeling from our make out sesh. Hot Boy Matt kissed me. Or should I call him Funny Hot Sexy Matt? Is that too many adjectives?

"Jo?"

"Hmm," I say in way of acknowledgment. I don't have words to speak right now. I'm too relaxed. Too happy.

Matt chuckles before saying, "Should we make our way to the party?"

"But this is so nice. You, me, nature. Emphasis on the you and me." I lift my head off his shoulder and give him a very exaggerated wink.

"You're ridiculous," he says with affection clear in his voice, and it nearly melts my heart.

"Okay, then, let's go." I pretend to start making moves.

"Hey, hey, just a few more minutes." And before I know it, we're kissing again. I can get used to this.

* * *

Matt and I are strolling hand in hand to the bus stop when we hear someone yell his name.

"Matt!" A shorter guy with an athletic build jogs toward us.

"Oh, hey, man, what's up? It's good to see you!" Matt lets go of my hand and extends it out to his friend to do that bro-hug thing guys do.

"I'm good, man! I'm actually heading over to my sister's apartment for a party. Where are you going?" His eyes dart toward me.

"Oh, yeah, we're also going to a party. This is Jo, by the way. Jo, this is my friend, Baker, from my hometown. We grew up together."

I shake Baker's hand and as I'm doing so, I notice Matt giving me a look. I'm not sure what he's trying to tell me.

"Nice to meet you!" I smile genuinely. Baker seems nice.

"You, too!"

The bus pulls up and the three of us get on.

"So, where are you two going?" Baker asks.

"We're going to a surprise birthday party!" I say enthusiastically. I'm actually excited for this party, now I'm on cloud nine from our kiss...or should I say *kisses*?

"Oh, that's cool. Which apartment are you guys headed to?"

"The Rose, I think... right, Matt?" I look at him, and he's shaking his head at me, trying to tell me something. What am I missing?

"Um, maybe... I'm not exactly sure which apartment we're going to. Let me look." Matt pulls out his phone and starts typing.

A few seconds later, I get a ping on my phone and see I have a test from Matt. That's strange. I open it.

The party we are going to is a surprise party for Baker!

I clamp my hand over my mouth and try to hold back the laughter I feel bubbling in my throat. The person we were going to a surprise party for is standing in front of me.

I look over at Matt, who is avoiding my eye contact—probably because if he looks at me he'll start losing it.

"Finally, this is our stop. Got to go, see you around, Baker!" Matt stands quickly and grabs my hand, ready to get off the bus as soon as possible.

"Oh, hey, man, this is my stop too!"

Uh oh, of course, it is. We're going to the same place.

"Oh, no way..." Matt trails off.

We all get off the bus and Baker says, "I'm going this way. Where are you headed?"

Matt points in the opposite direction. "Oh, we're going this way. See you later, Baker!"

Baker waves and sets out on his way. When he's at least thirty feet away, Matt pulls me into the nearest store—a deli.

We both burst into laughter.

CHAPTER 8

———

"You're not very good at keeping secrets, are you? Remind me to never let you plan a surprise party!" Matt says, teasing me while we're huddled in the corner at the front of the deli.

"Hey! In my defense, I had no clue who Baker was, and you never told me the name of your friend whose birthday we were going to!" I put my hands on my hips and paste a pretend scowl on my face, but it's hard to keep it there too long with Matt around. My face spreads into a wide grin. "It was pretty funny though."

"It was hilarious! I swear, I thought I was going to burst out in laughter on the bus."

"Poor Baker. I hope we didn't ruin his party for him."

"He seemed pretty oblivious to me. We'll just have to show up at the party after they yell surprise. We have some time to kill." Matt turns away from the window and toward the deli. I follow his gaze.

For the first time since we stumbled into this place, I'm finally seeing it. Booths line each side of the restaurant. The tables have a vinyl red and white gingham pattern on them. Even though this place is called a deli, it seems more like a diner. Dark wood panels line the walls and give the place a cozy feel, even if it does look a little dated.

And then it hits me. A waft of the most delicious-smelling Thanksgiving dinner you could ever imagine. Turkey, stuffing, sweet potatoes, and gravy, all rolled up into one. My mouth starts to water.

A middle-aged woman with her hair twisted in a large clip and an apron tied around her waist pokes her head out from behind what looks to be the kitchen door and says, "Hi, there. Take any table you'd like and I'll be right out."

I turn to Matt. "I don't know about you, but I can always eat."

"I'm so glad you said that. I'm suddenly starving. Whatever they're cooking back there smells amazing."

We pick the booth closest to us and sit down. Within minutes, the woman is at our table. "Hiya, my name is Mimi. What can I get for you two cuties?"

It sounds like it would be weird, someone calling a couple of teenagers "cuties," but coming from her, it seems motherly and reminds me of home.

"Something smells amazing. I want whatever that is," Matt says, basically drooling at the mouth.

It makes me laugh.

The woman chuckles. "Believe it or not, you're not the first person to ever say that! It's our signature Thanksgiving Sub. It's a hot sandwich with dinner-style sliced turkey, stuffing, cranberry spread, and gravy."

"That sounds incredible!" I'm at the edge of my seat. Food makes me very excited.

"We'll take one!"

"Do you want any sides? We have all the Thanksgiving fixins you could think of."

Matt and I look at each other with the same expression on our face: *Could this night get any better?*

* * *

Fifteen minutes later, our table is filled with little bowls of Thanksgiving side dishes, and we each have half of the sub in front of us.

"Are you ready?" I ask Matt.

"I have never been more ready for anything in my life."

"Okay, on the count of three, we take a bite. One...two... three!"

Matt and I each take a bite of our sandwiches.

"Oh my God." This is all I can say; I'm too consumed by this food.

Matt nods. "Best. Sandwich. Ever."

"I don't even care that you almost ruined Baker's surprise party. I think it was fate. We were supposed to eat this sub tonight."

I laugh. Even though it sounds totally ridiculous, I feel the same way. "This may be the best stop of the night!"

Matt puts down his sandwich. "Wow. I've been shown up by a sandwich. Is this what my life has come to?"

"If it makes you feel better, the garden is a close, and I mean, *really*, close second." It's too easy to joke around with him.

He laughs. "You're a character, Jo Prescott." The way he says it, I know he means it in a good way.

"Thanksgiving is my favorite holiday. My parents always host it at our house. We have like, thirty relatives over and it's total chaos. But I love it." It makes me excited to think that Thanksgiving isn't too far away. "What's your favorite holiday?

"Christmas Eve is my favorite night of the year. My Italian side of the family does the feast of the seven fishes. We cook all day and eat until midnight."

"That sounds nice, minus the fish."

Matt seems shocked. "What's wrong with fish?"

I can't help but laugh at the defensive tone in his voice. "It smells...fishy."

A smile spreads across his face.

I can't help but ask, "So, you're close with your family, huh?"

"Yeah, they're the best. Don't know where I'd be without them."

It makes me happy to hear him say that. "I like that. It's something we have in common." A shy smile flutters across my face.

"Me too." He smiles back.

We spend the next few minutes devouring our food. I didn't even realize I was that hungry.

The waitress makes her way over to us. "How was everything?"

"Awesome. I am officially stuffed," I say.

"Me too! Totally worth it," says Matt.

"Should I even ask y'all about dessert?"

"None for me, thank you. I already have enough of a food baby as it is!" *Oh, my God, did I just say that out loud?*

"All right, you two. Well, here's your check. Come around again soon."

Mimi seems sweet. I can picture myself becoming a regular here. Sitting in a booth, studying, drinking a hot chocolate, the smell of Thanksgiving wafting through the air.

I'm pulled out of my daydream when Matt says, "You ready to go?"

"But we have to pay." I rummage around in my bag, looking for my wallet.

"My treat." He slips a twenty in the little black book and he holds his hand out for me.

"Thanks. You know, tonight has been a pretty good night."

"I'm glad." He smiles at me, and warmth spreads throughout my body. "Now, let's go to this party!"

We leave the deli hand in hand.

* * *

All the buildings that line Main Street are alive at night. Bright lights shining through the windows and music blaring so loud the street feels like a club. The ground literally vibrates from all the excitement.

Matt gently pulls my hand with him as we enter a tall brick building. It must be twenty floors. We step into the elevator with a few other people and press the button for the fifteenth floor. I don't know why, but I'm starting to get nervous. This is the *real* first college party I've been to. I'm new to all of this.

"You okay?" Matt asks.

"Is it that obvious I'm nervous?"

"Nah, not at all." He's just being nice. He gives my hand an encouraging squeeze. "It'll be okay. I won't let you go, remember? Scout's honor."

And that's enough to settle my nerves.

We step off the elevator and head toward what seems to be the loudest door in the hall.

"Should we knock?"

Matt looks at me like what I said is the most endearing thing in the world.

"What?" I ask.

Instead of answering with words, Matt leans his face down and kisses me. He lets go of my hands and molds his hands to my face. My heart accelerates and that familiar tingle runs down my spine.

I can't help myself—I put my hands on the back of his neck and pull his body closer to mine. After what feels like mere seconds, Matt pulls his face from mine and I'm disappointed, but not for long. His lips start planting kisses from my collarbone, up my neck, along my jaw, and then they find my lips again.

"Matt," I say in a hushed tone, one of need. Lust.

He chuckles under his breath, but there's no humor in it.

"Oh, hello! Looks like there's some fun happening out here!" someone says.

I immediately push Matt away from me. I must look like a deer in headlights. I start pulling down the edges of my shirt where they were riding up, and I try my best to catch my breath. Matt seems to be catching his too.

The person who opened the door and scared me is already walking down the hallway, like they walk in on people making out all the time.

I point a playfully accusing finger at Matt. "You're dangerous!"

"I can't resist. You look too good."

I blush. "Damn, you're good. Let's go to this party already. I've been waiting all night!"

"Ladies first." Matt gestures for me to go into the apartment, so I do.

It's dark in here except for two strobe lights and a bright light-up neon sign that says *Party House*. There are so many people here. There's barely anywhere to walk and the music is *loud*. Another level loud.

"Baker!" Matt shouts. He takes my hand and pulls me along with him.

"Dude! What are you doing here?" Baker looks slightly stoned and a lot drunk.

"This was the party we were coming to all along!"

"What?" Baker's shouting now. "What did you say?"

"I said this was the party we were going to all along!"

"No way! This is a party for me!"

Matt just laughs and holds his hand out to Baker. They do another one of those bro hugs. Baker looks happy. So does Matt.

Instead of yelling more, Matt gestures to Baker that we're going to get drinks.

"Okay! See you later!" Baker shouts back to us.

Matt and I make our way into the cramped kitchen. Matt passes me a beer and grabs one for himself. We clink our drinks and I take a sip. Beer isn't my favorite, but what can you do?

Matt takes my non-beer hand and leads me to the dance floor, aka the living room. An Avicii remix is blaring through the speakers, and we start scream-singing to "Wake Me Up" and jump up and down to the beat like everyone else.

College is fun.

DAY 31

CHAPTER 9

The sun pours through the window so bright it wakes me up. I'm not even mad about it. I'm so, so happy. Last night was one of the best nights of my life. A funny, smart, hot boy likes me. And I like him.

I stretch my arms over my head and check the time.

1:00 p.m.

Oh, my God, I slept so late! For a second, panic washes over me, until I realize that it's Saturday. I snuggle into my bed and grab my phone.

Scrolling through, I see a text from Ginger:

Are you awake yet? I want to hear about last night! Plus, BRUNCH!

Oops, that was from an hour ago, so I quickly text her back.

Sorry! I'm up now! Brunch?

Then I see a text from Matt. My heart squeezes with delight just at the sight of his name.

I had a great time last night. :)

It makes me smile. I'm about to start typing back when the door swings open. Becky.

My good mood is replaced with anxiety, anger, and annoyance. I clench my fist around my phone.

I don't think I'm ready to have a confrontation with her. I just wish she wasn't here right now, killing my awesome post-date buzz.

Deep breaths, Jo, you got this.

I decide to just walk past her and head to the bathroom to start my day.

But then she does something that surprises me—and maybe even herself. She drops her bag dramatically and turns to me. "Jo, I've had enough of this! I'm sorry about the vomit thing! I don't want us to be those roommates who hate each other and stay away from our room to avoid one another. It's exhausting."

Wow. The apology I've been waiting for. Well, kinda. Sounds like she's more upset that she can't be comfortable in her own room than anything to do with me, but she has a point. I definitely don't want to deal with this awkward tension forever, but I don't really believe she's going to make an effort to be nicer to me.

I don't know if it's from the high of my date last night or what, but I say, "It's not just about the vomit thing. You haven't exactly been nice to me." I don't bring up the shirt yet.

Becky isn't even taken back. It's like she's already rehearsed for this, "I know, and I'm sorry! Sometimes I just get wrapped up in myself."

I'm not convinced, but I'm ready to be done with this conversation. "Okay, I accept your apology."

She smiles and claps her hands. "Okay, so now that that's settled, let's go out tonight!"

Uh, what? Is this girl crazy?

"Oh, come on, Jo! It will be fun! Abby and Ellie are coming over to pregame in a few hours. I'll even do your hair and makeup for you!"

"I don't know, Becky. I'm not really in the mood."

"It will be good for us to hang out together!"

Should I do this? Should I go out with Becky and her friends? One of which I really don't like?

She's holding out an olive branch, and I should take it. Right? I mean, it's just one night. Maybe it will get her off my case. I'm definitely having a lapse in judgment when I say, "Fine."

"Yes! Oh, and since you don't have any good going-out clothes, I'll have Ellie bring you some options. You guys are about the same size."

"Thanks." I need to get away from her. To think. "I'm going to grab food. I'll see you in a few hours."

"K, bye!"

And just like that, I've sealed my fate with the devil.

* * *

"Ginger!" I practically whine as I knock on her door.

I hear footsteps behind the door. Please, let it be Ginger.

My purple-haired best friend opens the door. Relief washes over me and, without thinking, I hug her.

"What's up with you?" she asks.

I ignore her question. "I'll buy you brunch. I have a favor to ask."

"Oh, no. Here it comes."

"Will you come out with me...and Becky and her friends tonight?" I rush through the second part.

"I thought you hated them?"

"Technically, I never hated anyone. Just felt a strong annoyance toward them. And not all of them! Just two out of three."

"Why, then?"

"Becky kind of apologized. And she asked me to go out tonight. I thought it would make our living situation a little better if I did this with her."

"I don't know. If you can't stand her, I won't be able to! I have a much lower tolerance for bullshit than you do."

"Please, Ginger. I'm asking you as my friend. You're the only thing that will make this better!"

Ginger grabs her keys and slips on her shoes. "You owe me. Starting with brunch."

"Thank you, thank you!"

To soften her up, I tell her all about my night with Matt.

* * *

After brunch, Ginger and I take our time getting back to the dorms. She knows I don't want to spend too much of the day with Becky, but when we finally get back, I know it's time to put my game face on.

"For the next few hours, Becky is going to do my hair and makeup."

"Oh, girl, I do not envy you."

"How about this? You fake an emergency and then we don't have to go tonight! We can just watch Netflix and order takeout. That sounds so nice. It's the perfect chilly fall day for some comfort food."

"Don't you remember? You were the one who asked *me* to go out tonight! Anyway, it'll be fine, don't try to get out of it now. It's one night. We can order takeout tomorrow."

"You're being really cool about this," I say, a little surprised.

"I haven't really gone out yet since I've been here. It'll be a new experience. Gotta look at the positives."

"Whatever makes you want to come tonight, I'm grateful! I guess it's time for me to get beautified by the roommate." I roll my eyes, not looking forward to this one bit. "See ya later."

"Good luck, girl."

When I walk in my room, Becky is waiting. She has all of her makeup, brushes, and other tools lined up on her desk.

"Oh, good, you're back! I was starting to get worried. I'll need a good bit of time to work on you."

Lovely, a nice insult to start of this torture. Taking a deep breath, I walk over to my desk chair and sit down. "Be gentle," I warn her.

"I'm not going to hurt you. Just relax."

Becky gives me two hours of her famous "beauty treatment" before she finally says I'm ready. Two hours full of face masks, eyebrow plucking, nail painting, *lots* of makeup, hair curling, and Becky's 'Get Pumped' mix, which mostly consists of Drake and JLo. The eyebrow plucking sucked but everything else was actually fun. I have no clue what most of the stuff she put on my face even was.

Becky didn't let me see myself the entire time she was doing my makeup. I had to sit in my desk chair facing away from the mirror. I'm sure if I had seen the process, I would have told Becky to stop thirty minutes ago. I usually just wear mascara. It's not that I don't *need* makeup; I'm just not confident using it. The first day of high school, I experimented with eye shadow—bad idea. It looked like someone gave me two black eyes. Since then, I've kept my makeup routine very simple.

With a few excited claps, Becky says, "All right, I'm just about done! Are you ready to see the new and improved Jo Prescott?"

In the most deadpan voice I can muster, I say, "I'm as ready as I'll ever be."

With that, Becky turns my chair around and I look at the person staring back at me. I can tell it's me, but a bolder version of me...a more enhanced version. My eyes are bright and a more intense green than usual. My lids are a plum color with black eyeliner and my eyelashes are thick and long. My eyebrows look clean cut for once in my life, and my skin is vibrant and warm with some subtle shine under my eyes. My blond hair is in relaxed waves down to my shoulders; it looks full and shiny. I can't believe it. I move my hand to my face to see if it still feels like my face.

As I'm lifting my hand, Becky slaps it away. "Don't touch your face! That's the first rule of makeup. If you touch your face, you'll ruin it. I think we better put some setting spray on you, just in case."

Becky starts rummaging through one of her many makeup boxes and pulls out something that looks like hairspray and points it right at my face. I flinch and she says, "Close your eyes."

I obey and a cool mist hits my face. It actually feels extremely refreshing.

"Done. So? What do you think? You haven't said anything!"

"It looks...wow. Great."

"I know, right? I made you a babe!"

Backhanded compliment number two of this experience. It doesn't even bother me this time. Who cares?

Without much else left to say, I reply, "Thanks."

It took Becky two hours to transform me, but it takes her about twenty minutes to do her makeup. She doesn't need to do her hair because it's already perfectly wavy. She sprays some perfume and puts on a skintight bright pink dress that barely covers her butt.

As she's slipping her heels on, the door swings open and it's Abby and Ellie. Abby is holding up some big plastic cheap-looking bottle of vodka with a huge smile on her face. "Let's get drunk!" she screeches.

I've never seen her this excited. Meanwhile, I'm the total opposite—extremely nervous about what this night will hold.

CHAPTER 10

I'm in a daze sitting on my bed as this scene unfolds around me.

"Hotline Bling" blasts over the speakers in our room as Becky grabs a stack of red solo cups from the top shelf of her closet. The next thing she grabs is a couple of bottles of blue Gatorade from our mini-fridge. I always wondered what those were for. I just thought Becky really liked the stuff. I guess it's just a mixer.

Abby's in charge of mixing drinks, which makes me nervous. Something tells me the ratio of these drinks will be 50 percent vodka and 50 percent Gatorade.

I'm pulled out of my trance of watching Abby pour drinks when Ellie taps me on the shoulder.

"Jo, we need to pick out your outfit for tonight! I couldn't get a sense of your style the other day, so I brought options just in case." She goes into her bag and pulls out three hangers.

"There's this." Ellie shows off the dress as if she's a cheesy car saleswoman, using one hand to hold up the garment and the other waving over it with a flourish. "Here, we have an olive green, mid-thigh length dress."

What Ellie doesn't mention is that it's also very tight and revealing. I don't even know if my boobs would fit in that dress. This dress is a version of the same one Becky, Abby, and Ellie are all wearing.

"Pass." At first, I feel a little rude for being so blunt. But you know what? I'm not wearing something I won't feel comfortable in.

Ellie says, "Okay...what about this?"

She pulls out a black bandage skirt that looks so tiny it would barely cover my butt. I raise my eyebrow at her. "Pass."

"You're not going to make this easy, are you?" she says and playfully rolls her eyes.

"I'd say I'm sorry, but I'm not. I don't like tight clothes." I shrug my shoulders. Ellie isn't bad.

"Then I think you'll like this one. It's the last thing I brought, so you better like it. It's just a top, but I thought you could match it with jeans." She gives me a hopeful smile and holds up a deep red velvet tank top with thin straps and a slightly plunging V-neck. It reminds me of the top Becky ruined.

Heat rushes to my face, and I can't help but think about the moment when I found my shirt, crumpled at the bottom of Becky's hamper, a stain across the front.

"Jo?" Ellie waves her hand in front of my face.

Blinking my eyes, trying to settle my rage, I say, "I'll take it."

Ellie lets out a sigh of relief. "I was starting to think you wouldn't like anything I brought you."

She hands me the shirt and I turn away from the girls, take my T-shirt off, and slip the tank over my head. I rummage through my drawers, grab the black skinny jeans I wore the night before, and pull them up my legs as quickly as I can. The whole time, I'm still thinking of the incident with Becky.

"Oh, my God, you *would* wear a bra with that shirt." Abby laughs loudly.

My fists clench involuntarily, and it takes all my strength to relax them. I'm not going to let them get to me. Not tonight.

I don't want to give Abby the satisfaction that she was right, but this top does look silly with bra straps. Dammit. Begrudgingly, I unclasp my bra and slide it from under my tank and throw it in my closet.

"Here, we can tighten the straps," says Ellie. I still don't understand why she's helping me when she's friends with these two.

The door cracks open. It's Ginger.

"Ginger!" When the others aren't looking, I mouth "thank you" to her as I make a prayer sign with my hands.

She squints her eyes at me and gives me the "I'm watching you" gesture, making me laugh. The others look up and I give them an angelic smile.

"Everyone, this is Ginger. She lives next door. Ginger, this is my roommate Becky and her friends, Abby and Ellie."

"Hey," Ginger says with a small wave.

"I love your outfit," says Ellie.

I couldn't agree anymore. "Damn, girl! You look hot!" She's rocking a vintage-looking Rolling Stones T-shirt with the front tucked into a short leather skirt and combat boots to complete the look. Her dark outfit really makes her lavender hair stand out.

Ginger's cheeks turn a light shade of pink. "Thanks."

Abby walks over with a mischievous smile plastered on her face and two drinks in her hands. "Here you go, ladies. We're gonna chug these."

Ginger drinks hers immediately and hands the cup back to Abby. "Can I have another?"

Abby gives Ginger an approving look. I'm a little shocked. Ginger and I have never partied or gone out together, so this is a first.

Quietly, she says, "What? If I'm going to survive a night with these girls, I need to be drunk."

I whisper back, "You're right."

Abby hands Ginger her new drink, and Becky and Ellie join us in the middle of the room with their drinks.

"To college!" yells Becky.

We cheers, clinking our cups together and all join in. "To college!"

As expected, the drink is mostly vodka. The burning liquid sits in my mouth and I force myself to swallow it. It burns on the way down and then feels sort of good. Before I know it, Becky is taking our cups and making our second round of drinks—the third for Ginger. I hope she puts a little less vodka in them than Abby did.

"Okay, let's play truth or dare!" Abby exclaims.

Does this girl love to torture me or something? "How about I just tell you I'm a virgin instead of you putting me on the spot?" I say, feeling bold and honestly tired of their games. I don't care if they know, but these stupid truth or dare games always turn into people asking about sexual experiences or who's done what drug. I hate it.

"Sweet, innocent Jo. You didn't have to tell us that. I can see it written all over your face," Abby says, acid thick in her voice.

I'm fuming. I can't stand these girls.

Becky hands us our drinks, and I immediately take a long swig. Ginger looks at me with a look that says, "Damn, girl." I shrug and hold my cup up to her. "Cheers." We clink cups. I take Ginger's advice and get drunk.

"Before we start, I have a twist to the game. I like to play where you can ask any question you want to the person, not just one that has a yes or no answer," Abby says.

"You're kidding me." Is this girl for real?

"That's the way we're going to play."

"Cool, can't wait," I say, sarcasm heavy in my voice. At least I'm actually starting to feel a buzz, thank God.

"Jo, you're first. Truth or dare?" Abby looks at me like I'm a toy to play with.

"Truth." If this girl wants to play, I can play.

"Who do you think is the prettiest of all of us?" She smirks to herself and takes a sip of her drink, like she's really proud of her question.

Without a second thought, I say, "Ginger."

Ginger smiles at me, and Abby rolls her eyes. I have no allegiance to these girls, except Ginger. I'm not letting this jerk come between me and my best friend.

"Now you ask someone, Jo," says Becky. She seems annoyed.

"Okay." I look around the room and spot Ellie. "Truth or dare, Ellie?"

"Dare!"

Hmm, I was too busy thinking of Becky's reaction to think of a dare.

"I dare you to...chug the rest of your drink." Not very original. Oh, well.

Ellie obliges and finishes her drink. She smiles. I think she liked that dare.

"Truth or dare, Becky," says Ellie.

"Dare," says Becky with a mischievous smile on her face.

"I dare you to go outside and invite the first boy you see to come play with us."

Becky immediately stands up and sets her drink down with purpose, like she's on a mission. With a flip of her hair, she's out of the room.

I take my phone out to text Ginger.

Can't wait for this night to end. Thanks again for coming 🙏.

Ginger's phone audibly pings. She pulls her phone out of her pocket, but her movements seem a little disjointed.

"yeh don t foregettt you owee me. foOd... my pick."

Ginger's tipsy! I laugh. Whatever gets her through tonight.

Becky pushes open the door with someone following behind her. Actually, it looks like a couple guys. The first is tall with blond hair in a man bun on top of his head. He has pale skin and bright blue eyes. He's staring at Becky like he's never seen a woman before in his whole life.

As Becky and man bun guy enter the room, I see who is behind him. Matt. My heart immediately drops.

CHAPTER 11

———

I put my cup to my lips and tip it back. Of course, with my luck, I drink it too fast and start coughing. Great, already drawing attention to myself. Ginger starts hitting my back, trying to help me stop coughing.

Everyone's looking at me. How embarrassing.

"I'm good," I croak, giving everyone a small smile. I catch Abby smirking at me, and I narrow my eyes at her—no use pretending I like her.

Becky says, "Ladies, this is Mateo." She gestures to man bun guy. He barely takes his eyes off her as he pulls his hand up to wave at us. This dude is mesmerized by Becky. "And this is Matt."

I smile up at Matt and warmth spreads throughout my body, and no, not just because of the alcohol. My memories of last night flit through my brain, and I blush at the thoughts. But seeing him with Becky reminds me of what I saw that first night here at PSC. For weeks, I've been repressing the memory of seeing Becky on top of Matt, making out. She hasn't mentioned him and he hasn't mentioned her, so maybe it was nothing...a girl can hope.

Sometimes, I just can't help but stare at Matt. This is one of those times. He looks perfect in a plain, dark green T-shirt, jeans, and a pair of Adidas. As I'm doing a once-over on his appearance, I finally find his beautiful face, and he's looking right at me.

Feeling brave and also annoyed at the thought of Becky near Matt, I get up and give him a soft kiss. As soon as our lips touch, the soft, sweet kiss turns into something more. Matt's kissing me back, and his hands find my hips to pull me closer.

I'm not sure how much time passes when Becky clears her throat. I try to pull my face from Matt's as fast as possible, but he gently puts his hands on either side, smiles at me, and whispers, "Hey, 409." I practically melt at his words. I love when he uses my nickname.

I keep my hands on his sides but pull my face back so I can look at him. I look up through my eyelashes and smile weakly.

Something dawns on me that I probably should have thought about sooner. "What are you doing here?" I whisper, not wanting everyone to be a part of this conversation.

He chuckles and gives me a big smile and hugs me back. He leans close to my ear and says, "I missed you. I was coming over to surprise you."

I smile as his words tickle my neck. He was coming to see me. The euphoria doesn't last long when I realize what he has just walked into. A night out with Becky and her friends. I glance in her direction and she looks pissed. Shit...

Becky plasters a fake Stepford-wife smile on her face and says, "Come sit, guys, and I'll pour you drinks."

As I think about Becky's shift in attitude, I return to my seat on the floor.

I feel someone sit next to me and know it's Matt before I even look at him. It's so cute that he wants to sit next to me, but what will Becky think? I'm already worried that real daggers will fly at my head from Becky's eyes, not just the metaphorical ones.

Forgetting about her for a second, I let my eyes settle on Matt. I stare at his hazel eyes, his nose, his lips, just studying his face. *Why, oh, why, did he have to be with Becky that day?*

"Jo?" Matt saying my name is enough for me to come alive and forget my worries at least momentarily.

I say the first thing that's on my mind, not thinking. "You have nice eyes. They're the perfect mix of brown and green." And just like that, we're having a moment, like no one else is here.

A smile spreads across Matt's face and a soft chuckle leaves his lips. "Thanks, I get them from my mom." He pauses and looks at me. "You have nice eyes too."

Our spell is broken when Becky hands Matt a drink. *Note to self—don't be all into Matt in a room full of people! Especially one with Becky.* I don't really want to be her friend, but I don't want to upset her. We're just starting to work things out and start over. I don't want it to be awkward between us anymore.

I pat the floor between Matt and me and say, "Becky, come sit!" There's an immediate pang in my chest. Ugh. Why did I do that? I don't want her near Matt. My heart is screaming at me. It aches. My brain is telling me to be rational. But when emotions are involved, nothing is rational, right?

Those daggers I mentioned earlier? Yeah, they are coming straight from Becky's eyes into mine.

She sits down, crosses her legs, and turns to Matt, leaving her back facing me. Yup, instant regret. I suddenly feel a lump forming in my throat. I focus my eyes on the floor to compose myself when I feel a hand on my shoulder. Ginger. What an angel.

Ginger stands up and says, "I'm going to go to the bathroom, you want to come?"

I silently thank Ginger with my eyes and nod because I don't think I can speak without crying. I stand up, wipe the dust off my butt, and put my drink on the desk as I follow her into the hallway. As I'm passing through the door, I sneak a look back into the room. I see Becky touching Matt's arm and whispering something in his ear. I think I catch Matt looking at me, concern on his face, but I rush out of the room as soon as I see how close Becky is to him.

* * *

Ginger pulls me into the bathroom, back in the place where I first met her. It seems like an eternity ago, but it's only been a few weeks.

"Are you okay? Wait, before that...damn, girl! Full on make out sesh in front of everyone? I'm impressed! And a little grossed out," Ginger says, trying to lighten the mood.

Her distraction works, and a laugh escapes my lips. "I know, who am I? It was just supposed to be a quick kiss! But that boy's lips are dangerous." I grab a paper towel to wipe the few tears that had a chance to escape my eyes. I don't feel like crying anymore. I'm more annoyed than anything.

Ginger chuckles. "Okay, so what happened back there? Becky's claws were out."

"There's something I never told you about Becky...and Matt." I pause and take a deep breath. "On move-in day, after we met in the bathroom, I went back to my room and caught Becky straddling some guy, making out. Turns out some guy was Matt."

"Damn, girl."

"I know. I didn't know I'd have class with him or end up falling for him! I haven't had the guts to bring it up. I'm too scared."

Ginger stays silent.

"C'mon, Ginger, I know you have an opinion on this. I want to hear it." As much as it will hurt.

She holds up her finger, telling me to wait. She's thinking.

My insecurities get the best of me. "I know Becky is hotter than me. She's got that whole tall, thin, beautiful thing going for her. And what do I have going for me?" I start to panic. Why does Matt like me? *Does* he like me? "I'm spiraling, Ginger!"

Ginger comes over to me and puts her hands square on my shoulders. "Take a deep breath, Jo, and listen to me. Matt is not interested in Becky. Watching you and Matt just now, it seemed pretty obvious he was interested in *you*. I mean, we all watched your tongues touch, it was gross! He likes you!"

I blush and begin to speak before Ginger cuts in, "Whoa, whoa, whoa, I said listen to me." I'm a little shocked at Ginger's forceful tone, but it makes me realize she doesn't take any crap. I kind of like that, because she genuinely cares about my well-being.

I close my mouth and listen. "Good. Sure, Becky is tall, thin, and beautiful." So much for my self-esteem. "But you can't compare yourself to her. You're beautiful too."

I shrug at her, not convinced.

She continues, "In middle school, I remember looking at other girls in my grade, who went through puberty and started using makeup. I looked at them and thought, why can't I have bigger boobs or be taller or have perfect eyelashes? I came home from school one day crying about it. My sister took my hand and said something that has stuck with me since that day. She said, 'Envy is the thief of joy.'"

She pauses momentarily, maybe waiting for me to respond. She goes on, "It means that jealousy will steal your happiness. The best thing any of us can do for ourselves is to accept who we are."

I sit quietly for a minute and let Ginger's words seep into my brain. I repeat the wise words in my head. "It's not easy to change your whole way of thinking and feeling."

She smiles mischievously at me, and I raise my eyebrow at her.

"Okay, I have an idea, you're going to hate it." She turns me toward the mirror in the bathroom and says, "Repeat after me," with a huge smile on her face.

She starts, "I'm Jo Prescott, and I'm amazing!" She shouts the last word. "Okay, now your turn."

I turn beat red and look at her in the mirror. "You've got to be kidding me."

"Oh, come on, have some humility. It'll be fun!" she says.

"I'm Jo Prescott, and I'm amazing," I say, with embarrassment seeping through every word.

"Nope, not good enough." Ginger crosses her arms in front of her chest and stares me down.

I let out a nervous laugh, but do it anyway. "I am Jo Prescott and *I'm amazing!*"

A girl I've never seen before walks in the bathroom and goes past us to the stalls. I look over at Ginger and we both start cracking up.

"Wow, that was actually extremely cathartic. You're a smart cookie, Ginger Yu!" I nudge her shoulder and say, "Now it's your turn."

"We both already know I'm amazing." She smiles at me and threads her arm through mine. "Let's get back. They're probably wondering where we are."

I roll my eyes at Ginger, but really I'm just thinking about how lucky I am that I met her.

* * *

We push the door open to my room and see everyone is standing now and huddled in a circle.

Ellie hears us come in and shouts, "Gingerrrr, Jooo! Time for a shot, then we're going downtown." She's pointing both hands at us and doing some sort of weird swivel movement like she's dancing. Wow, I didn't realize how drunk Ellie was. It's actually kind of funny. She hands us our cups with about an inch of vodka in them.

We join the group in the center of the room. My mirror affirmation with Ginger, paired with the alcohol, is making me confident. I raise my cup and say, "To PSC!" The others raise their cups to meet mine, we clink, and down our shots. It burns, but I smile through it. Maybe tonight won't be so horrible.

Then my eyes land on Becky's, and she quickly looks away from me to Matt with a smirk on her face. Panic washes over me. What is she going to do? And just like that, the unsettling feeling in the pit of my stomach is back.

Our little group is making our way down the hallway to the elevator when I realize I didn't bring my bag.

"Shoot," I say under my breath and stop in my tracks. I turn to Ginger. "I left my bag in the room. I'm going to run back. Can you come back with me?"

"Sure, let'ssss go," says Ginger. I stifle a giggle. When I wasn't looking, this girl got drunk!

"We'll catch up with you guys downstairs. I left something in the room," I tell the group.

Becky acts like she hasn't heard me, and I think the others are too drunk to care.

Ginger and I start walking back to my room. We walk a few steps before I realize someone is following us. I look back and see it's Matt.

"What are you doing?" I ask.

"I thought I'd come with you two. The girls were talking about Mateo's man bun…a conversation I don't need to be a part of."

"Oh, okay." I'm shocked and pleased Matt chose to come with Ginger and me instead of staying with Becky and the girls.

We reach my door and Ginger says, "I have to pee, I'll be right back." She winks at me—the kind where her mouth is open. She thinks she's being sly, leaving me and Matt alone. My brain is immediately panicking but I try to keep it cool on the outside.

"Hurry back, Ginger!" I say.

Matt and I walk in my room, the door quickly closes, and it's very apparent we're alone.

I spot my bag on my bed, grab it, and put it over my head in one swift motion. "Okay, good to go!" I say, hoping we can just wait outside the bathroom for Ginger so I don't have to be alone in my room with Matt.

But Matt's looking at the photos on my wall. Particularly one of me and my family from the morning of my high school graduation. I'm in my cap and gown and I'm sandwiched between my parents and brothers. Mom looks like she's about to burst into tears of happiness, Dad looks stoic as usual, Ben is smiling brightly and pushing Ollie away with his hand behind my back, Ollie looks disgruntled and is giving Ben a mean side eye, and I'm just smiling, glad I finished high school.

"Are these the brothers you were telling me about the other day?" Matt asks.

"Yup, that's them." I smile at the picture and start to feel emotional. I miss my family, now more than ever.

Matt takes my hand and leads me to my bed. We sit on the edge, my hand still in his. "Are you okay? You left so fast earlier. I got up to find you, but I thought it'd be weird to go into the girls' bathroom."

"Yeah, I'm fine. I just...seeing you and Becky together, when I don't really know..." I don't know how to finish my sentence and ask what I really want to ask. My internal voice is screaming at me, *what's going on with you and my roommate?*

His face falls; he knows what I'm getting at. "I know we haven't talked about it... about you walking in on us the day you got to PSC. But I want you to know there is nothing between her and me. It's kind of hard to explain."

I'm intently listening to Matt's every word, finally about to get an answer about him and Becky, when Ginger abruptly makes her entrance into my room and startles me. I jump up and accidentally stomp on Matt's foot.

"Oh, my God, I'm so sorry, Matt!" I put my hands to my mouth. I'm so embarrassed.

He winces. "It's okay. It's okay. I've had worse. Four sisters, remember?"

Ginger actually seems oblivious that she just walked in on something. "You two ready to go? I want to get to the party before I have to pee again."

As we head downstairs, all I can think is that I almost got the answer to the question gnawing away at me for weeks. What happened between Becky and Matt?

CHAPTER 12

We're nearing the edge of campus when downtown PSC comes into view. It's dark out but I can still see all the local businesses that line Main Street. A running store, a diner, and a few PSC clothing stores. I make a mental note to myself to come here in the daytime when all these stores are actually open.

As we get closer, it gets louder and I notice hundreds of people walking up and down the street in groups, trying to get to their next party location. Most of the girls are dressed in low-cut tops and short-shorts or tight dresses. The guys all look very college—some in button-down shirts, some in PSC shirts, but all of them seem to be in some sort of khaki pants or jeans.

We make our way across the street and become part of the crowd of party-goers. I grab Ginger's arm tightly so I don't lose her in this chaos and look around to make sure Matt is still nearby. He takes one look at me, and I think he can tell I'm nervous. He reaches over and grabs my other hand. Like every time Matt touches me, my heart skips a beat. As I stare at my hand in Matt's, I forget we're surrounded by masses of drunk people.

Matt speeds up our pace and we make a hard left turn down a side street. He drops my hand but I'm still holding onto Ginger. Disappointment washes over me at the loss of his touch but I look around us and realize we are away from the crowd, and my disappointment is replaced with relief.

"First time being downtown on a Saturday night can be tough to navigate. Over the summer, it was half as busy as it is now and it was still wild. Sometimes it helps when you're drunk." Matt gives us a weak smile.

I feel a pang of jealousy. The idea of Matt being here over the summer and drinking with other people—other girls, especially drunk girls in tight clothes—makes me a little uneasy. I can't compete with that.

"Let's go to the party." I change the subject, not wanting to think any more about Matt's summer.

Matt nods back and turns to walk up the street.

I glance at Ginger, who seems to be enjoying herself, and pull her along with me up the street. "Come on, girl, let's get you to this party."

A few minutes and hundreds of drunk people later, Matt says, "Here we are."

The small house with cobblestone siding looks like a cottage you would see in a quaint little town. There are string lights along the walkway and in the trees on the front lawn. It's beautiful.

As we near the house, it's impossible not to hear the loud music and vibrations coming from within.

Matt pauses before opening the door. "You ready?"

I nod and he pushes it open.

I scan the party. The place is packed! There must be a hundred people in this tiny place. Twinkling string lights are draped across the walls, just like the outside of the house.

There's a wall covered with beer boxes, like wallpaper. Not as cute as the lights, but I guess this *is* college.

Country music fills the house. It's not the type of music I'd imagine at a party; at least not a party I'd ever been to, which isn't saying much.

"I'll get us some drinks," says Matt, breaking my trance. He leans in close to me and whispers in my ear, "Don't go too far, I'll be right back."

I get goosebumps up my arm. I smile up at him and say, "Okay."

"Come on! Let's go look around." Ginger tugs on my arm.

"Okay, okay!" I hold tight to her arm. I don't want to get lost in this party by myself.

We make our way through the living room and see a group of guys playing beer pong. On one side there are two guys dressed in preppy clothes and look intense as they play, like their lives depend on this game. On the other side of the table are two guys dressed casually in T-shirts and shorts, who look totally at ease with the game. My bet is on the latter pair.

We continue past the game of beer pong and I notice a door to the backyard. Curiosity gets the best of me, and I pull Ginger with me outside.

The backyard also has string lights, but this time they're on the surrounding trees, creating an awning of lights above us. Whoever lives here must really like these little lights. They *do* make the place feel a little more magical and a little less like a college house.

People are scattered throughout the backyard, but to our right a group is gathered in a circle around something.

Ginger notices the group too. "Let's check it out."

As we get closer, we see the group is huddled around a tree stump.

"What are they doing?" I ask Ginger.

"I'm not sure, maybe they worship tree stumps in Pennsylvania?"

We both break out into a fit of laughter. I feel like one of the reasons Ginger and I get along so well is that we grew up in the same area. Being in Pennsylvania sometimes seems like another world.

"Hey, what are you girls laughing at?" one of the guys from the circle shouts.

"Oh, no, we've been caught," says Ginger and starts to giggle.

I'm glad she thinks it's funny; I couldn't be more embarrassed. My face heats up, and I hope they didn't hear Ginger's comment.

Instead of answering the guy's question, Ginger starts walking toward the group. "What are you doing?"

The guy meets us halfway and says, "We're playing a game called stumps. You two should join. I'm Peyton."

Peyton has dark brown curly hair, pale skin, brown eyes, and a nice smile.

I'm about to open my mouth to introduce myself when Ginger cuts in. "I'm Ginger! This is my friend Jo. We'd love to play." Her voice sounds perkier than usual.

I'm sensing a vibe between these too. Does Ginger think Peyton is cute? She's getting all...not Ginger. Giggling, smiling, blushing—who is this girl?

"Cool! So, the point of the game is to hammer your nail in first, but there's a twist. You have to throw the hammer in the air, catch it, and then hit your nail. Even before a few beers, this game is hard."

"You play this game while you're drunk? It sounds dangerous." I can't believe I said that. What a lame thing for a college kid to say.

Peyton starts laughing in an easygoing way. "That's why it's fun! Come on over."

Peyton leads us back to the circle and introduces us to the group. "Everyone, this is Ginger and Jo. They're going to join this round." I give a shy smile to the group.

"Okay, let's start already!" one of the girls in the group says. She looks very determined.

I whisper to Ginger, "I'm going to go to the bathroom. I'll be right back, okay?"

Ginger nods but I can tell she's barely paying attention to what I said. She's staring at Peyton.

Before going inside, I turn back to look at the game. Maybe I can catch Ginger's turn. She's holding the hammer and Peyton has his hand wrapped around hers. He's standing closely behind her. She must be loving that!

Seeing Ginger with Peyton makes me think of Matt. I wonder where he is.

I'm passing the beer pong table on my way to the bathroom when I hear, "Hey, red tank top!"

Are they talking to me?

"Yeah, you!" I look up to see one of the casual beer pong guys pointing at me. I feel my face heat up. What could this guy want?

"You want to take a celebrity shot for me?" he asks.

"What does that mean?" My heartbeat's accelerating.

"You've never played beer pong before?"

I shake my head no. I mean sure, I've seen people play it before, but I don't know the rules.

"We're about to fix that. A celebrity shot is when someone outside of the game takes a shot for the person playing. I picked you for my celebrity shot, so you're going to throw this ball and try to get it in one of their cups." He smiles at me. "Got it?"

"I don't have very good hand-eye coordination. Maybe you should pick someone else?" I start to walk away.

His hand lands on my shoulder, "Hey, not so fast! Come on, just give it a try."

"Okay, fine." I grab the ball out of his hand and, without hesitation, throw it in the direction of the other cups. To my surprise, it goes in. I throw my arms around beer pong guy's neck and hug him to me. "Oh, my God, I did it!"

His arms snake around my back and he squeezes me tightly. I instantly realize I'm hugging a total stranger, and I peel my arms off of him. "Sorry about that. I don't know why I did that."

"No complaints here. Great shot by the way." The way he says it creeps me out. I push myself away from him but he holds on tight.

"Hey, come on, stay and watch me play." He has his hands around my wrists now and I'm trying my best to break free of his grip.

Panic mixed with anger swirl inside of me. Who is this creep? What gives him the right to hold me like this? Someone interrupts my thoughts.

"Get off her!" It's Matt, and he's pissed.

My creeper is momentarily distracted by Matt. Fueled by anger, I knee him in the groin as hard as I can. Casual beer pong guy immediately falls to the floor and curls up into a ball.

A group of people are staring at me. The music is still playing but all the background noise has completely stopped, like the party just halted to watch the spectacle. The seconds tick by slowly as my embarrassment grows.

Someone starts to clap. Matt. He's smiling at me, and I'm relieved. Within seconds, everyone around me is clapping and whooping.

I give a shy smile, take Matt's hand, and drag him with me to the backyard. People from the crowd are patting my back like I just hit a homerun. I think I've had enough attention for one night.

"Wow, I was ready to beat that guy up and then POW, right in the kisser! Well, not exactly in the kisser." Then he starts cracking up.

"I gotta be honest, that felt amazing! I can't believe I did that!" Adrenaline rushes through my veins.

"It was pretty incredible to watch. That guy had it coming."

"I thought creeps at parties were just cliches in movies. Guess not."

A few moments pass when Matt says, "I think you need a drink." He hands me a red solo cup full of purple liquid. It looks like Kool-Aid.

"What is this?"

"Jungle Juice. It's pretty much a lot of alcohol and juice. It's super sweet but packs a punch, so be careful."

I chug the entire thing and pass the cup back to Matt.

He takes the cup and shakes his head, chuckling. "Let me get you some water. Stay here, I'll be right back."

The alcohol mixed with my adrenaline high from earlier is making me antsy. I'm just going to go hang out with Ginger and the stump people until Matt gets back.

Ginger has an intense look on her face with a hammer in her hands. She throws up her hammer, catches it, and with what looks like intense force, slams her hammer down into the stump and misses her nail by a hair. Peyton throws his head back in laughter, and Ginger looks up at him with a scowl on her face.

I tap Ginger on the shoulder as the next person takes their turn. She still looks annoyed, but when she sees it's me, she smiles. "Hey! Where have you been?"

"Oh, around." I give her a wicked smile.

"What did you do?"

"I'll tell you later. I'm starving!"

"Peyton was telling me about a pizza place open late. Wanna go?"

Peyton chimes in, "It's the best drunk food!"

I chuckle. "Sure! I just have to find Matt."

"I'll meet you up front. I need to say bye to some people," says Peyton.

Ginger and I make our way through the house to find Matt.

What I see makes me stop dead in my tracks.

Matt has his back against the counter near the sink, and Becky stands in front of him, with her hands on either side of him, leaning on the counter and as close to Matt as she can get.

I audibly gasp and Matt's head snaps up. "Jo, it's not what it looks like!" Matt tries to push Becky out of his way, but I don't stick around long enough to see if he's successful.

I elbow my way through the crowds of people, trying to get away as fast as I can.

CHAPTER 13

I pull the wooden door open with as much force as I can muster and run up the street. I don't want to look at the cobblestone house. I don't want to hear the music. I don't want to think of anything that has to do with the party or this night.

My legs take me to the park I saw on our way to the party. The park is simple; just a slide, some swings, and a rickety old seesaw surrounded by a small field of grass. No one is here, which is just what I need. I sit down on one of the swings and gently sway forward and back. My mind races a million miles a minute.

What did I walk into with Matt and Becky? Are they secretly together or something? I feel so stupid. I should have stayed away from Matt. I knew something had happened between them, and I don't even know what. My heart aches. I really thought Matt and I had something. Didn't we? Tears well in my eyes and a few spill over.

"Damn, Jo. You're…fast. I have to catch…my breath." Ginger makes her way into view.

I wipe the tears from my eyes, hoping she doesn't see. Guilt washes over me for making a scene and making her run after me.

Ginger takes the swing next to me and gently sways. Her breathing starts to slow; I think she's recovering. "You will never make me run after you ever again! You know I hate physical activity!" She swats her hand across my shoulder.

I deserve that. If I didn't just see one of my nightmares play out in real life, I'd probably laugh at her swatting at me—but nothing feels funny now.

"You're right. I'm sorry." I sound so pathetic.

"I'm not really upset at you. I was trying to lighten the mood. Clearly, that was the wrong approach."

I don't say anything. I don't feel like talking. I just feel like wallowing in my own self-pity. Wow, I'm pathetic.

Ginger and I silently sit on our swings, swaying for a while, and I'm grateful. Maybe it's because Ginger knew I needed some silence. Or maybe she doesn't know what to say either.

There's a slight breeze tonight and the sky is clear. I can see every single star in the sky. "You know, I think this is the first time since I got here that I'm actually sitting still. It's a beautiful night. Peaceful." Sitting here in the park, away from the crowds of people, you would never know it's a college town. It reminds me of home.

"I know what you mean. It feels like we've been in the college bubble for a long time. There's been one thing after another since the moment we stepped foot on campus."

"Yeah. I don't know how I'd be getting through any of this without you."

"Same."

We smile at each other. Then Ginger asks me the one thing I've been dreading. "So, do you want to talk about what happened back there?"

I take a deep breath. "If I'm being honest, not really."

"I gave you some time to think. Now it's time to talk it out."

She's right. "I know I only met Matt a month ago, but there's something between us. Every time I'm with him, I feel like every cell in my body comes alive. He makes me laugh, he makes me smile—plus, he's super hot."

"Super hot," Ginger echoes.

"But there's this thing with Becky. He hasn't told me what it is. He almost told me tonight, you know. When you were in the bathroom. But someone interrupted us." I look pointedly at Ginger. I continue before she can protest. "Seeing him with her tonight, it brought all my insecurities rushing back. I don't know if I can be with him if he has some sort of connection with Becky. Maybe it's not worth it."

"That's a decision you have to make. Either way, maybe it's worth hearing him out. Hearing his side."

"Maybe. I need time to think. Time away from it."

"Well, if you need a distraction..." Ginger hops off the swing and pulls me off mine. "Let's get pizza! It's food for the soul. And if anyone's soul needs food, it's yours."

I put my arms around Ginger and hug her close to me. "Thanks, girl."

"You're welcome." She squeezes me back, which shows a lot, because I know Ginger isn't a hugger.

* * *

I wait at the park while Ginger goes to find Peyton in the front yard of the party. I feel an ache in my heart as my mind wanders to thoughts of Matt. Where is he now? Did he go back to the party, back to Becky? Is he looking for me?

"Earth to Jo!"

I snap my head up, Ginger's voice breaking my reverie.

"I thought we lost you for a minute there," says Peyton with a chuckle. I like that Peyton is already comfortable joking with me. He seems carefree but genuine.

The five-minute walk to the pizza place is filled with a debate between Ginger and Peyton about who's the best character in *The Office*. I mostly just listen, not really in the mood to chat.

"It's clearly Dwight. I can't even believe we're having this argument!" says a begrudging Ginger. "He has the most quotable lines of anyone else in the show! Think of all the memes!" Ginger's throwing her hands in the air to make her point more convincing.

Peyton puts his hand in a prayer pose like he's thinking. "Ginger, I respect your opinion, I do. But Michael Scott *is The Office*. Come on!"

"What do you think, Jo?" Ginger asks.

Damn, I was barely listening. "Uh. Ginger's right." Who was she even talking about?

Ginger has a triumphant look on her face and sticks her tongue out at Peyton. He's not giving in so easy. He starts right back in on the debate, and I go back to not paying attention.

"We're here, ladies!" Peyton smiles and holds his arms out wide in front of a grungy, rundown pizza place that has a line of about fifty people outside.

It doesn't look that special. I must have made a face, because Peyton says, "Oh, come on! It's a dollar a slice, you can't beat it. Plus, look at this line. Long lines mean good food. It's just a rule of the world."

I barely notice Peyton says the same thing I say to Ginger all the time. I'm too in my feelings right now to say anything.

"I don't care what it is, I'm starving. This line better move fast," says Ginger as she clutches her stomach.

Ginger and Peyton's debate has now moved on to *Parks and Recreation*. I pretty much tune them out and take a look around. Across from the pizza place is an old-timey ice cream shop and, a few blocks down, an Indian restaurant. There are frat houses lining the street. Hordes of people make their way to the various houses, all loud and clambering on top of one another.

Before I know it, we're almost at the front of the line. I go to grab my wallet out of my bag, but Peyton holds his hand up. "It's on me tonight." I'm about to protest when he says, "It's just a few dollars. Don't worry."

Ginger has this goofy smile on her face as she stares at Peyton. Damn, this girl has it bad. Peyton is cute in a nerdy yet adorable way. I can see why Ginger is crushing on him.

We get to the counter and order four plain slices: two for Peyton and one each for Ginger and me. We grab a spot at one of the wooden tables outside.

I take a bite of pizza. I didn't realize how hungry I was. This pizza is nothing like New York-style pizza. It's too doughy and the sauce is so sweet. Is this what Pennsylvania thinks pizza is?

I look to Ginger because I know she's probably thinking the same thing. She has a smirk on her face.

"It's not very good," I say matter-of-factly.

"That means you're not drunk enough. Or you have high pizza standards. Which is it?" Peyton asks.

I'm not really in the mood to talk, but I have to defend my city. "I'm from New York. I'm used to good pizza."

"Sounds like a pizza snob to me." He says it in a way that makes me know he doesn't really think I'm a snob. He's just joking.

"Jo's right, this pizza isn't very good. But damn, was I hungry." We all look down at Ginger's empty plate and laugh like it's the funniest thing in the world. It's cathartic.

* * *

"Where are you both living?" Peyton asks.

"Lackawanna Halls."

"Cool, I live in McKean. We're heading in the same direction." Peyton gets up and throws out his paper plate. "You ready?"

"Yeah, let's go. I'm ready for bed." Ginger winks at Peyton. If I didn't seen it with my own two eyes, I wouldn't believe it.

The flirting between these two has definitely ramped up since we first got to the pizza place. I don't think I can handle much more of it, especially in my achy-breaky state.

"So, where is McKean?" I ask, trying to break some of the sexual tension between these two.

"It's on the Northwest part of campus, to the left side of the student union building."

"Cool."

On our walk toward campus, I notice the streets are thinning out. It's much less crowded than it was earlier tonight. It's quiet—peaceful, even.

"Hold on." Peyton puts a hand on my shoulder and Ginger's and pulls us back a few steps. "Look. Isn't it beautiful?"

In front of us is the oldest building on campus, Davis Manor. It's sort of a historic monument and symbol of the university. It almost looks like a castle or building you would see in *Downton Abbey*. It's made of brick and has ivy growing up the sides and sits on a vast lawn of perfect green grass. It's beautiful, especially with the moonlight shining on it.

"Wow. It's perfect," Ginger says, awe clear in her voice.

"This is where you get to spend the next four years. It's the best place on Earth. You're going to love it here." Peyton is still looking at campus when he says this to us. I can tell he's lost in his own thoughts about life here at PSC. I hope he's right, because right now, all I feel is heartache.

DAY 32

CHAPTER 14

——

I turn over in my bed and lazily open my eyes. It's bright in our room but the sun isn't shining. It's overcast. My head is throbbing. I feel like I have a hangover, but I wasn't even tipsy by the time I went to bed.

Last night, Peyton walked Ginger and I back to our dorm, and before he left, he gave us a big dimpled grin and with his arms wide open said, "Welcome to PSC."

Even though I wasn't in the best headspace last night, there was something about that moment. I don't know what it was, but I knew it was something that would be ingrained in my brain forever. It felt like a positive omen, but I don't really know why.

Later that night, when I was walking to the bathroom to brush my teeth, I saw Ginger letting Peyton into her room. Not really sure why they're trying to sneak around; maybe because Ginger doesn't want to rub it in my face. Or maybe because they like being sneaky. I'm happy for Ginger; I'll have to ask her for all the deets later.

I'm startled from my thoughts when I hear Becky snore loudly. I don't even remember her coming in last night. I got back before her and pretty much went right to bed, exhausted from the events of the night.

I don't know if it's because it's a new day, fresh start and all that, or if it's because of Peyton's encouraging words about PSC, but I don't feel the heavy weight on my chest I've felt in the past when I think of Becky and Matt together. I don't want to be that girl who pines over a guy she's only known for a few weeks, especially one who potentially has something going on with someone else.

With that thought, I spring out of bed, energized at my epiphany. I put on my running gear and slip out of our room so I don't wake the beast—I mean Becky.

Campus is quiet, dead even, after a Saturday night. Everyone is probably still asleep or nursing a hangover.

I take a few deep breaths and start on my run.

Even though I've been here for over a month, I'm still not very familiar with campus. I mostly just go straight to the buildings I have classes in and to the library to study. Today, I just run where my feet take me and they eventually take me back to Davis Manor.

I stare at the historic building in awe. It's almost as beautiful in the daytime as it is at night. Being here, looking at this building, feels special. PSC feels special.

Instead of doing my normal post-run stretches, I lay down in the grass and close my eyes. The sun has come out and the overcast sky has disappeared.

"Can't get enough, can you?" I open one eye and look at the direction of the voice. It's Peyton. I smile up at him.

I close my eye again and take a deep breath in. "You've created a Davis lawn monster."

I feel him sit down near me. "The only thing I've done is introduce you to the best spot on campus. I think I've given you a little bit of the PSC magic."

"I'll give you that." I sit up. "Thank you. Something about your optimism about PSC, seeing how much you love it here, and even the crappy pizza, reminded me why I wanted to come here in the first place."

"How so?"

"When I came on my tour back in high school, I remember the vibe here being so energetic. All the students had a love for this place. I think I've been too nervous, too in my head since I've gotten here. I forgot this is the place I want to be."

"Glad I could help. It's not easy adjusting. I didn't always love it, and then one day things just changed. I think it takes some getting used to."

"Definitely." I smile. I like Peyton. He better treat Ginger right.

"You hungry? Let's get Ginger and go to brunch."

"That sounds perfect." I'm glad I have a new friend in Peyton.

* * *

As we round the corner of my dorm building, I hear someone calling my name.

"Jo! Hey, Jo, wait up!" I stop. It's Matt.

He jogs up to where Peyton and I are standing. The blood drains from my face. I don't think I'm ready to talk to him yet.

"Hey," I say, trying to sound calm.

Matt looks from me to Peyton, a curious expression on his face. A little part of me wants him to be jealous, seeing me with another guy, but the other part of me would never want Matt to think something was happening with Peyton. So to clear up any confusion, I say, "Matt, this is Peyton. Peyton, this is Matt. Ginger and I met him last night at the party. We crossed paths on my run this morning." Dear God, why is this so awkward?

"Hey, nice to meet you," Peyton says.

"Likewise." Matt smiles at Peyton but it doesn't reach his eyes. He's suspicious.

There's a weird silence I'm not really sure how to fill. Poor Peyton has no clue what's going on, but maybe that's for the best.

Finally, Matt says, "Jo, can we talk?"

My cowardice takes over. "Peyton and I were actually just on our way to wake up Ginger. We're going to brunch." Matt looks visibly hurt, and I instantly feel a twinge of regret. I quickly add, "Maybe we can meet up later?"

"Yes! That would be great! I'll meet you at our spot. Seven o'clock?"

An emotional spasm runs through my body when Matt says "our spot." Memories of our Friday night date at the dome flash through my head, and I wish things were that simple. I do my best to muster up a smile. "Sounds good. See you later."

"Later." Matt moves closer to me and gives me a gentle hug and whispers in my ear, "I promise to explain everything." He slowly releases me, looks into my eyes with such sincerity it hurts, and turns to leave.

I momentarily feel a glimmer of hope, I want to believe nothing is happening between Becky and Matt...but I need answers.

* * *

"Who was that back there?" Peyton asks as we ride the elevator up to get Ginger.

"Just a friend," I say, not sure I want Peyton to know all the drama that ensues in my life.

Peyton tries to stare me down but I avoid his gaze. I'm not getting into this right now.

Changing the subject, I say, "So should I wake Ginger up or should you? She's not very happy in the mornings."

"In that case, you. Definitely you."

We finally make it to my floor and I knock on Ginger's door. There's no sound or movement coming from behind the door, so I push and find it unlocked.

I quietly creep into Ginger's room. The smell of fruity bubblegum fills the air. I keep forgetting to ask Ginger what air freshener she uses, because it smells amazing.

Ginger's sound asleep. I almost feel bad before I get a running start and leap onto her bed.

"What, what's happening? What's happening?" A shocked Ginger opens her eyes, and I'm smiling down at her.

"Time to wake up! Brunch is almost over, and we're hungry."

Ginger picks her head up off her pillow and looks past me at Peyton, who is trying to look innocent.

Ginger blushes; maybe I should have had Peyton wait outside. I probably wouldn't want a boy I like to see me when I first wake up. There's usually lots of drool involved.

Ginger finally says, "I would be pissed at you right now, but I love brunch, and I don't want to miss that. Give me five minutes."

"Cool, we'll wait outside," says Peyton.

"Actually, I'm going to go to my room and change. I'll be quick. I'll meet you outside in a couple of minutes." I scoot out of Ginger's room and into mine.

I let out a sigh of relief when there's no sign of Becky. I find a pair of sweatpants and my comfiest sweatshirt and slip them on. I grab my wallet and notice Becky's phone sitting nearby. The screen lights up. I don't know what comes over me, but I pick up the phone. I instantly regret my decision.

A text from "Matt <3" lights up on her screen.

I take a deep breath, trying to stay calm. Maybe it's a different Matt.

I still have Becky's phone in my hand when I hear the creak of the door open behind me.

"What are you doing with my phone?"

CHAPTER 15

——

I slowly face Becky. She's in a towel with her wet hair dripping on the floor, her hands on her hips, and her eyes filled with fury.

Seeing her ignites my own fire.

"Matt texted you," I say, trying to keep my voice steady.

Becky strides across the room with purpose and snatches her phone out of my hand. "Oh, did he?" she says with a smirk on her face.

In this moment, I hate her. Before I can think of something to say, Becky continues. "Let's just see what he said. *I had a great time last night, can't wait to continue where we left off,* winky face. That's adorable. We did have a great night. I forgot how soft his lips were."

The blood drains from my face. Is that true? Did Matt and Becky end up hanging out last night after I left the party?

"That's not true. Matt and I…Matt and I are…we're…" I stammer.

"Are what? Together?"

I stare blankly at Becky, not sure what to say. What *are* we? We've never really talked about it.

"Oh, Jo, oh, honey. That's cute. Let me assure you, you and Matt were and are *nothing*."

"You're lying." Tears are threatening to spill down my face.

"I know Matt better than you do. I spent all summer with him."

It's like a glass has shattered. Summer semester. Matt and Becky were both here this summer. How did I not see this before? It makes so much sense.

I'm still in denial. "That day I walked in on you two together, you said you had never met him! That he just came in the room and you started making out with him." As I'm saying the words, I realize how stupid they sound. Of course they knew each other.

"Don't be so naive. You heard what you wanted to hear. Matt and I have done things you probably wish you could get to do with him. We spent our nights drinking, hooking up, and having a damn good time."

"No." My lip is quivering now, and my hands are balled into fists at my sides, shaking from anger.

"Sorry to break it to you." But there was no trace of apology on her face or in her voice. She's loving every minute of this. This is the Becky who was hiding all along. "You think you're perfect with bright eyes and a cute smile, acting like you're so innocent. Let me tell you something, I see right through your act. Matt is mine, so back off."

And that's when the tears start to fall. I push past Becky and make my way out of our room as fast as I can.

* * *

"Finally! We're starving out here. What took you so long? Jo, what's wrong?" Ginger is at my side in seconds when she notices the tears on my face. Anyone seeing me right now probably thinks I'm having a mental breakdown; maybe I am.

I'm relieved to be outside, in the fresh air and away from Becky, but the relief isn't as strong as the sinking feeling in my stomach. Pain, anger, and sadness. I drop to my knees and sit on the grass, suddenly feeling too tired to stand.

"Becky and Matt..."

"You talked to Matt? What did he say?"

"No, not Matt. Becky."

"What did she say?"

"Matt texted her. He said he had a great time with her last night."

"Oh."

"They were together over the summer. They knew each other from summer semester. I can't believe I didn't figure it out on my own. It was right in front of my face the whole time."

"How would you have known? Matt should have told you."

I shake my head. "I feel like an idiot. I shouldn't have started something with him."

"Jo, don't say that. You're not an idiot!"

A few moments pass by and I realize I'm keeping them from food, so I let them off the hook. "I think I just need to be alone for a while. Maybe go for a walk and let my mind process this."

"What about brunch?" asks Peyton, hopeful. I feel bad for making him witness this mess I've become. He looks uncomfortable, but hey, he's still here. He must really like Ginger.

"You guys go. I'll catch up with you later."

"Jo." Ginger's expression tells me she's a little hurt and a lot worried.

"Don't worry, I'll be fine. Just need to clear my head. Promise. I'll text you later."

I head downtown, not looking back. I can't stand to see Ginger's expression any longer.

* * *

I make my way past the main street on campus and just walk, wandering here and there and nowhere in particular. After fifteen minutes of my aimless journey, I end up at the park from last night. I sit on the swing and start pumping my legs lightly, gaining a slow speed.

I let my mind wander and try to make sense of everything that has happened since I've been at PSC. I met Becky and immediately got bad vibes. She's friends with Abby! What a big red warning flag I ignored. But I didn't think she could be so cruel. I didn't know anyone could be so cruel. I didn't know real Mean Girls even existed.

I think of Matt and the first time I talked to him—so sweet, funny, and cute. He makes me laugh and smile. He's close with his family. But...he and Becky. I should have known that day I saw them together in my room. As much as it hurts, I need to stay away from him.

No more Matt. No more Becky.

I'm going to focus on me.

I send Ginger a text.

Thai delivery later and The Office? Girls only?

Within seconds, I get a text back.

YES! I'm hungry just thinking about Pad See Eew.

Before leaving the park, I silently vow to myself that I will not let this get me down. I have friends who support me and a family who loves me. Everything else is secondary.

* * *

Ginger opens the door, expecting me with a look of pity? Concern?

"I'm fine, Ginger! I promise. I did some good thinking this afternoon. I'm not going to let this get to me. I'm starving! I can't wait for Thai food any longer."

"Okay." Ginger doesn't seem extremely satisfied with my answer, but hey, she can't argue when it comes to food. "You're in luck, because I ordered ahead. It should be here any minute."

"You're my savior." I wrap my arms around Ginger and squeeze her tight.

"I'll let this hug slide because I know you're having a rough day. But after today..."

I let go and chuckle to myself. "I'll send you money."

I pull my phone out and see the time on my screen. *7:00 p.m.*

I'm supposed to meet Matt now, but I can't bring myself to do it. I turn off my phone. No more drama.

DAY 33

CHAPTER 16

———

Hey Jo, I'm here!

.

.

.

Are you running late? It's okay if you are...

.

.

.

Jo?

.

.

.

The next morning, I wake up and finally turn my phone back
on to find a string of texts from Matt. The last one came in at
nine o'clock last night. He waited two hours before he gave
up on me. Guilt washes over me for standing him up, and
sadness, knowing I can't be with him.

I stretch my limbs out from my makeshift bed on Ginger's
concrete floor. Staying here last night was better than the
alternative: potentially having to face Becky.

It's only six, but after seeing Matt's texts and lying on a concrete floor, I can't fall back asleep. Ginger's still sleeping, so being as quiet as possible, I fold up the blankets, write Ginger a note thanking her and letting her know I left to start my day, and tiptoe out of the room.

Before opening my door, I say a silent prayer to the universe, hoping Becky is asleep or not in our room at all. Relief washes over me when I walk in and hear her snoring. I guess it is really early; who, besides me, would be up at this hour?

It's ironic that Becky looks so peaceful in her sleep, so serene, but I know her true colors. Mean. Petty. Scary.

Anger boils up inside of me just thinking of yesterday. I realize my hands are balled up in tight fists at my side. I release them and take a deep breath. Why am I letting this person get to me so much?

With that thought, I change, pack my bag, and head to my favorite coffee shop on north campus.

* * *

"Large earl grey, please, cream and sugar." I pay the cashier and take a spot in an armchair facing the window. It's a cozy little nook, hidden away from the rest of the coffee patrons. I look at the yellow and orange leaves on the trees and the ground, lost in my own thoughts.

"Large black coffee, please."

I freeze. There's no way he can be here. It's too early.

"You look rough. How's it going?"

"I've been better. Rough is a good word for the weekend I've had."

"Rough weekend of partying?" the young guy behind the counter asks enthusiastically.

"Not exactly."

I slink down in my chair but peek my head over the side just enough to watch the exchange.

Oh, crap. It *is* him. My Matt. Well, not anymore. In all his beautiful glory. I shouldn't have looked, but now I can't look away.

The barista is wearing a confused expression on his face when our usual barista, Hank, walks out. Hank is an older gentleman who is always so sweet to me. He sometimes gives me a free scone with my tea and says it's because he can tell "I'm one of the good ones." Not sure what he means or why, but it always warms my heart.

Hank takes one look at Matt and then back to the younger barista. "This boy is having lady troubles. Can't you tell? He looks all mopey."

The younger barista replies, "Oh, sorry, man," and immediately walks away, looking a bit uncomfortable. I'm sure if Matt had said he was partying all weekend, he wouldn't have left.

"You have a good read on people, Hank, I'll give you that." Matt drops a dollar in the tip jar.

"So, what happened with your sweet girl? Let me rephrase: what did you do to mess things up with your sweet girl?" Hank has a stern look on his face, and I instantly feel my heart grow. At least Hank's in my corner.

"She kinda caught me with another girl." Hank's face becomes angry, but before he can say anything, Matt continues, "It's not what you think! This other girl, she can be aggressive, especially after she's been drinking. I was at the party with Jo and was just grabbing something from inside when this other girl cornered me. I didn't even want to talk to her. That's when Jo walked in." Matt's voice is unsteady; not something I've ever really heard before.

"I see," Hank says.

"I can't even imagine what it must have looked like to Jo. But it meant nothing!" Matt's voice is becoming panicked.

"Maybe you should try talking to her. Explaining?"

"She doesn't want to talk to me." Matt hangs his head.

I don't know if I can listen anymore. Everything Matt's saying is pulling me back in. Maybe what he's saying is true. Maybe it was a misunderstanding.

"Keep trying," Hank urges.

"Thanks, Hank. I'll see you later." With that, Matt's gone.

I know where he's headed next: the same place as me. Our one class together. I wait a few minutes before I leave the coffee shop, not wanting to run into him on my way there. On my walk, I contemplate what Matt said. Was the compromising position I found him in with Becky really that innocent? Let's be honest, nothing is innocent when it comes to Becky. She's evil. Well, maybe that's too harsh.

No, Jo, stop it! This is the drama we promised we would avoid. Whether Matt was telling the truth to Hank or not, it's not worth the headache anymore. I'm turning over a new leaf.

I check my phone and see it's a couple minutes past eight. I take a deep breath and hurry to class.

* * *

As soon as I step foot in the room, I spot Matt in his usual seat. I could find a place at the back of class, but decide against it since I've been sitting in the same seat all semester and it would be weird to move now. My inner voice tells me to not be a coward and just sit in my damn seat, but I'm still a coward because I avoid eye contact with Matt at all costs.

All during the hour, I try to figure out how to leave without Matt talking to me. I decide on the pack-up-early plan. I start packing up my things discreetly five minutes before class is supposed to end. This way, when it's time to go, I can just rush out.

My hand is wrapped around my backpack strap, ready to make a beeline to the door as soon as class is dismissed.

"All right, everyone, midterm papers are due *this* Friday. Do not forget! It's 25 percent of your final grade. See you in class Wednesday."

As the last word leaves his mouth, I stand up quickly and push in my seat.

Matt's faster. He's already packed up, has his backpack on, and is blocking my way out of class. "I saw you packing up five minutes ago, Jo. You forget that I know you."

We wait until everyone leaves, even the professor. As much as I wanted to get away, I don't want my private life to be public.

"I know you know me, but apparently not as much as you know Becky." I give him a small smile and try to get around him to no avail.

His voice seems softer now. "What happened last night? You said you would meet me." He sounds a little defensive but mostly upset. "I wanted to talk to you."

"Becky happened." I watch him closely, trying to gauge his reaction.

"I promise you, it's not what it looked like! There is nothing between me and her."

"You were together."

"We weren't! She—"

I cut him off before he can finish. "No, Matt, you were together over the summer. She told me."

Matt looks stunned.

I keep going. "Look, I don't want to get in the middle of anything with you and Becky. I have to live with her and based on what happened last night, it's not in my best interest to get on her bad side."

"Wait, did she...did she threaten you?" he asks, concern and disgust in his voice.

"No, not explicitly. Why didn't you just tell me?" My last shred of hope is hanging on the answer to this one question.

"Jo..." He pauses, thinking.

"It's okay, Matt. I'll see you around." I walk past him and don't turn back.

So softly, I think I imagine it, I hear Matt say my name, anguish clear in his voice. He sounds defeated. Has he given up? That hurts more than anything; more than Becky saying those things to me. Hearing him give up.

* * *

I usually kill my free hour in between classes getting coffee with Matt, but since that won't be happening, I decide to head back to my dorm and see if Ginger wants to go with me instead.

I make my way through our hallway and notice there are a lot more girls getting ready now. I've never actually been here at this hour. I hate waking up early some days but maybe it's a blessing. I wouldn't want to fight for a shower.

I give Ginger's door a couple soft taps. After a few seconds, I realize no one's coming. Maybe Ginger's asleep. I'll just wake her up. I push the door open and what I see is a shock to my system.

Ginger is making out with Peyton in her bed.

"Oops." I slap my hand over my mouth. *Shit! Did I just say that out loud?*

They both look up at me.

"Oh, my God, I'm so sorry." I put my hand up in front of my eyes, not wanting them to think I'm staring at them. "I, um, I'll just go." My face is hot with embarrassment.

I back out of the room and shut the door. I pace back and forth in the hallway. That was weird. Ginger and Peyton are rustling behind the door.

"Let me go talk to her. I'll be right back," I hear Ginger say.

Ginger steps into the hallway, closing the door behind her. "What's up?"

"Nothing! I was just going to see if you wanted coffee. No worries, I'll go by myself. I'm sorry I interrupted." I can't keep a straight face any longer. A fit of laughter takes over.

Ginger joins in.

It takes a few minutes to subside. I think laughing was the only way to overcome the awkwardness.

"So. You and Peyton, huh?"

Ginger gets quiet and blushes. "Kind of."

I'm happy for my friend. She's smitten. "Well, get back in there, girl! I want all the details. Later. Okay, bye!"

I give Ginger a quick hug and head back outside.

What now? I have no Ginger, no Matt.

I'm alone.

CHAPTER 17

——

I sit through most of my classes not even trying to pay attention. My mind just replays the last few days. Seeing Becky and Matt. Becky being a crazy bitch. Learning about Becky and Matt's past relationship. Ginger making out with Peyton. Me, suddenly alone.

After my final class of the day, I realize I have nowhere to go. I don't want to go to my room and face Becky the Beast. I can't text Matt. I don't want to bother Ginger; what if she's with Peyton?

So I do something different, something I've never done since being at PSC. I go to the student union. I've passed through a few times on my way to class as a shortcut, but never really hung out there. I hear there's a food court and that's enough to solidify my decision. I could use some comfort food.

Unlike Davis Manor, which is old and beautiful with ivy growing up the sides, the student union building or SU, as the students call it, is relatively new and modern. It was rebuilt only a few years ago, so everything inside and out is fresh. The floors are white and literally shine because the tiles have specks of sparkle in them. The main floor of the building has rows of long plastic tables lined with chairs of every color, some vending machines, and a plethora of fast food options. The ceilings are high and there are multiple floors, the upstairs ones are mostly meeting rooms for various clubs on campus. Or so I've heard.

I've never actually been on any floor except the main one. I usually just walk through the SU as a shortcut to get to my classes. Anytime I've ever walked through it was the middle of the day and it's crowded with hundreds of students trying to grab lunch or get to their next class as quickly as possible. But not now. It's actually pretty quiet, with small, scattered groups of students sitting at various tables. *Note to self, four o'clock is the ideal time to come to SU.*

Instead of staying in the main area with tables, I decide to explore a little. SU is huge and I have nothing but time, so I wander.

This place is definitely a lot bigger than I ever knew, with many different spaces for seating and never-ending hallways leading to different areas within the building.

My wandering has paid off. I've reached the holy land: Starbucks. I feel true excitement for the first time all day. If my eyes could turn into the heart-eyed emoji, they would. How did I not know there was a Starbucks on campus? At home, I used to clear my head by going to our local Starbucks, grabbing some sort of iced tea drink, or if I was really in the mood, a chai latte, and go for a drive. I don't have a car here, but I think the Starbucks will do for now.

"Black iced tea please...and a cake pop." I give the barista a big smile. She probably thinks I'm crazy. Does anyone get as excited as me when they order Starbucks?

I grab my drink and wander along the corridor, trying to find a seat. Armchairs line this part of the SU. The chairs are right up against floor-to-ceiling windows that face the south part of campus. They actually look pretty comfortable. I take a seat in the one in the corner, farthest from the other chairs.

For a few minutes, I just take in the beauty of campus, wondering what everyone else has going on in their lives. Maybe someone else is going through something like me. Or maybe they're all just "fun" college students.

I'm startled when a flier appears right in front of my face. I look up to see who's interrupted my trance. A tall guy with a flat-brimmed hat with red hair peeking underneath it looks down at me.

"Hey, I'm from the PSC student radio station. We're looking for new people to join. Our studio is just down there, near the Starbucks. If you're interested, just come by or send an email here." He points to the flier.

"Thanks, but I'm not a communications major," I say, a little disappointed.

"So?"

"I don't know, wouldn't you be looking for people actually studying radio or media or something?"

The guy chuckles. "Not everything in college has to be done because it's your major. You can do things for fun, you know." He leaves the flier on my lap and walks away.

My mind hangs onto one word he said. *Fun.* Isn't this what I wanted? I told myself today would be a fresh start, and here it is, being handed to me!

"Hey! Sign me up!" I shout loud enough so he can hear me.

He turns and beckons me over. "Come with me."

* * *

The station is completely run and operated by students. I learn about how 87.6 FM Power PSC works, from engineering, to advertising, to on-air talent. Before I know it, I've spent three hours in the radio station and it's eight o'clock.

The guy who recruited me, Jack, teaches me how to use the board. It's so interesting. He let me push some buttons and build a playlist. By the end of the night, I officially sign up to be part of the PSC radio team.

On my walk home, I'm on cloud nine. Who knew radio was so cool? I mean, I listen to podcasts like any other person my age, but have never really considered radio as some sort of hobby or even a club to join on campus. Everyone there seemed really nice, and Jack told me I have a voice for radio! I have to start by learning how to cut audio and create content for other shows, but in a few weeks, if I do a good job, I can have my own show!

This is my fresh start. This is something for *me.*

My head is reeling, I can't believe I stumbled upon this. I'm smiling to myself as I enter my dorm building.

Until this moment, I had completely forgot about the Becky and Matt drama. I slowly make my way up the stairs to my floor. Maybe I'll get lucky and Becky won't be there.

I must be lucky. Ginger is standing outside my door holding up two cartons of ice cream.

* * *

"I have a confession." I pause for fake dramatic effect. "I saw you letting Peyton into your room that night of the party. Tell me everything!"

"Oh, my God, it wasn't like that!"

I smirk at her.

"Okay, it was a *little* like that."

"Details, please!"

"Well, after you and I came back up to our rooms, I saw I had a text from Peyton."

"Go on." I say, egging her on.

"It said something about him forgetting something in my room and if he could come get it. But we both know he had never been in my room. I think it was his attempt at being cute and I couldn't help but laugh. Plus, I really wanted to keep hanging out with him, so I invited him up."

"Whoa, Ginger! You crazy girl!"

Ginger's cheeks turn a little pink. Ginger blushing? She must like this guy. "He came up here, and we just talked for hours. We like a lot of the same bands, and he wants to travel the world just as much as I do."

"Aw, that's really sweet." I'm so happy for her.

"Then we made out for a couple hours." She gives me a shy smile.

"Finally getting to the good stuff!"

* * *

Hours pass by and I finally decide to go back to my room. I can't avoid it forever. Avoid *her* forever.

There she is. Phone glued to her ear, talking at a decibel so loud it hurts my ears. She doesn't glance up at me when I walk in, but she says into the phone, "Oh give me a second, you-know-who is back." Then she laughs. A sinister, shrill laugh. Before I know it, she's gone.

Am I going to have to live in this hell for the rest of the year?

DAY 50

CHAPTER 18

———

"Okay, Jo. You're on in five, four, three…" Jack uses his hands to count down from two and then points to me.

"Hey, PSC, this is Jo Prescott and you're listening to 87.6 FM Power PSC. Stay tuned to hear some alternative pop and an interview with our very own Ed Rodgers, the man behind the mascot. As always, if you want to request a song, tweet us at PSC Power Radio." I turn off my mic as *Animal* by Neon Trees starts to play. The "Live" sign in our studio turns from red to white.

"Great job!" Jack is so encouraging.

"That was so cool! I can't believe I was just live on air!" My heart is beating at what feels like a thousand beats per minute. "That was such a thrill!" I can't believe how giddy I am. What a rush.

Jack chuckles. "Settle down, you have to go on again in five minutes to talk about upcoming events on campus."

"You should do it with me!"

"I don't know. I usually just operate the board."

"Come on, it will be fun! Plus, don't you want to be on this level?" I say gesturing to myself, hoping he can hear the levity in my voice.

Thinking for a few moments, he finally says, "Okay, let's do it."

Jack gets his mic set up, and I put my headphones back on. Jack counts me back in five, four, three...

"Welcome back to 87.6 FM Power PSC. In the studio with me is my good friend Jack. Say hi, Jack."

"Hi, Jack."

I can't help but crack up at his stupid joke. "That's Jack for you! Okay, so what do we have on tap for this week on campus?"

"I think a lot of people are going to be interested in this one, Jo. This Saturday at the SU, you can be a part of a Pokemon fashion show hosted by the gaming club!"

We spend the next five minutes riffing back and forth talking about current events on campus before signing off.

"That was so much fun!" I gush to Jack. My first day on the radio is one I'll never forget. "You were a great co-host."

"Co-host?"

"I'd be willing to make my show, *our* show. What do you say?"

Jack chuckles. "Sports are usually my specialty."

"Sports, shmorts! We make a good team. I'll let you have a segment about sports. I'll be uninterested the whole time; it will be a great bit!"

"I'll think about it."

Taking that as a yes, I say, "Cool! Let's meet before our next show to figure out what we're going to talk about. Bye, Jack, great job today!"

He shakes his head, and I leave the studio, making a beeline for Starbucks. Time to get my caffeine fix of the day.

I place my order and sit in one of the lounge chairs while I wait for my name to be called. I text Ginger to make sure we're still on for our study sesh this afternoon. When I'm not in class or at the radio studio, I'm usually hanging out with Ginger and Peyton. Today it will just be Ginger and me because Peyton is on a camping trip for the rest of the weekend.

"Hey, Jo."

I can already tell who it is by his voice. Matt.

"Hey." Damn, he looks good. He always looks good. I give him a small smile. I've been avoiding him after class.

The sad part is, despite everything, my heart still picks up its pace every time I see him. It's this other-level physical reaction. I can't help it.

"How are you?" he asks.

"I'm good. I joined the campus radio station."

"Really? That's awesome! I didn't know you were interested in radio." In typical Matt fashion, he rubs the back of his neck.

"Me neither, I just kind of stumbled into it. But I really enjoy it. How are you doing?" This feels so formal. So not us. Or what we used to be anyway.

"I've been okay. I'm sorry about everything."

I frown. I don't really want to do this now. "Matt, it's fine."

"It's not. And I know you don't want to talk to me so... I wrote you this." He pulls his backpack from his back and puts his hand in it, digging around for something. He pulls out a long white envelope and hands it to me. "It's a letter. Explaining everything. You don't have to read it, but I hope you do. I miss you."

I take it from him and look down at it. It says "Jo" on the front in what I'm assuming is Matt's handwriting. It's actually really neat.

"Black coffee for Matt!" the barista yells.

Matt zips up his backpack and slings it onto his back. "Good seeing you, Jo." He grabs his coffee and he's gone.

* * *

I venture up to the third floor of the SU. I want privacy to read my letter in peace. Lucky for me, there are lounge chairs on this floor, and it's a ghost town. I'll have to remember this spot the next time I need some quiet.

I rip open the envelope, eager to read what's inside.

Dear Jo,

First I just want to say how sorry I am. I should have been honest with you from the beginning and I wasn't. It's not because I didn't want you to know the truth, I just didn't know how to tell you...but that's about to change.

I want to start with the very first day I met you, the day you moved in. When you walked up to the welcome desk and referenced that Beach Boys song, I was hooked. It was so endearing, not to mention that the person saying it was a beautiful, blond, green-eyed girl who made my heart skip a beat. After I finished up at the welcome desk, I came looking for you. How could I forget what room you were in when you made it so easy to remember? 409.

Your door was wide open but I knocked just in case, I didn't want to be creepy. Then I saw Becky and wondered to myself, how could this be my luck? Someone from my past living with the girl who I wanted to get to know. You know Becky...she was pretty forceful and she started kissing me. You're probably thinking, "Yeah, right, he's a guy, he must have loved it." Trust me when I say, I didn't.

When I heard someone gasp, I was so relieved because it gave me a chance to (politely) push Becky off me so I could leave. Then I saw it was you. I couldn't believe it. I was mortified. I didn't even want to be with Becky, I had come to find you! In that moment, I thought any chance I had with you was gone. I did the only thing I could think of: get out of there as fast as I could.

I guess you're probably wondering what happened between Becky and I. We met over the summer and we became friends. She was pretty wild, partying all the time. She was nice enough and some of my friends were friends with hers. One night, she confided in me, something I don't think it would be right to talk about here. But I listened to her and tried my best to console her. She made a move on me and as politely as I could, tried my best to let her down gently. I just didn't think of her that way. I think it bothered her to be rejected.

When I saw you in class the first day of school, I honestly thought it was a sign of fate. It felt like the universe wanted us to be together. I think you felt it too. Instead of clearing the air that first day we got coffee, I chickened out. I was having so much fun hanging out with you and I didn't want to ruin it. I know now how big a mistake that was.

When you saw Becky and me the night at the party, it was nothing. Nothing, I promise. She was drunk and she cornered me. I tried to get around her, but I didn't want to push her out of the way. That's when you walked in. My heart sank. I couldn't believe my second stroke of bad luck. What must you have thought seeing us together *again? I went after you but couldn't find you. I made a promise to myself that night that I would tell you everything. The truth.*

I thought I'd get the chance to tell you when you agreed to meet me at the dome, but you never showed. I was crushed, but I understood. I can't help but ask, what happened that night? Why didn't you meet me? Was it because I hurt you too much?

I went back to my room and began writing this letter. I don't know if I'll ever give it to you because I'm a coward sometimes. But, if by some miracle you are reading this, it means I couldn't bear you not to read it. I need you to know the truth.

I'm crazy about you, Jo Prescott.

Yours always,
Matt

Tears fill my eyes. I can't believe a boy, *this* boy, wrote me such a beautiful letter, baring his heart to me. I can't help but wrestle with my own thoughts. His story doesn't line up with Becky's. But do I believe her or Matt? How do I know who's telling the truth?

I fold the letter back up, put it in the envelope, and stuff it in my bag.

It's time to confront Becky.

CHAPTER 19

———

Ginger and I are in my room, dressed in sweats with books and half-eaten bags of chips scattered around us.

I'm on edge and not because of finals. It's been weeks since I have hung out in my room, all in hopes to avoid Becky—but not today. Today I am ready for her. Ready to confront her.

Matt's letter told me his side of the story. It's time now to get the truth from Becky.

"Earth to Jo." Ginger waves her hand in front of my face.

I snap to attention. "I'm here! I'm focused."

"Then answer my question." Ginger has her arms folded across her chest.

"Can you please repeat it?"

She rolls her eyes at me. "What is the difference between classical and operant conditioning?"

Damn, our psych exam is a few weeks away, and I honestly have no clue what the answer is.

"Maybe we should order food. I can't focus right now. I think we need a break." Ginger gives me the *I knew you weren't listening* eye but I know once I mention food, she will be on my side.

"Fine, you know all my go-tos at our favorite places, so I trust you to order. I'm going to keep reading."

I'm about to hit "place order" when Becky throws open our door like a force to be reckoned with. My phone slips out of my hand and onto the floor. This is it. The moment I've been waiting for. To be face-to-face with Becky. My palms are sweaty in an instant and my heart is pounding in my chest.

Ginger reacts quicker than I do. She calmly closes her book and not so calmly stands up and throws the book on the floor. Ginger knows all the details of the Becky and Matt debacle.

"I know you don't really know me, but I don't stand around letting people bully my friends. Who do you think you *are*?" Ginger puts her hands on her hips and stares at Becky.

"*Excuse* me?" Becky crosses her arms and stares just as menacingly at Ginger.

Even though I'm so grateful I have a friend who is willing to stand up for me, I can't have Ginger fighting this battle—but seeing her so quick to defend me reminds me I have true friends who support me. Because of that, I can do anything. I can do this.

I calmly stand up and walk between the two of them. "Ginger, it's okay. Really."

Becky looks triumphant, which bothers me, but I know I have to keep my cool. "I do have something to say to you, though."

"This should be good." She's trying to provoke me, but I won't let her.

"Look, Becky, if I know anything about myself, it's that I'm a nice person. I go out of my way to try and be nice to everyone. I may not be the smartest, prettiest, most athletic, artistic, or whatever, but I know I'm a good person and I don't deserve the way you you've been treating me." Becky tries to say something, but I hold up my hand, signaling her to let me finish.

"Whenever someone has been mean to me, whether it was a rude customer at work or a friend who may have snapped at me, my dad would remind me that I don't know what's going on in that person's life. There was likely something going on with them I had no clue about."

"What are you getting at?" Becky scoffs, venom in her voice.

"I don't know what's going on in your life, and that's partly my fault. I never really took the chance to know you. I was intimidated from the moment I met you—tall, tan, and beautiful. I shouldn't have let that stop me from getting to know you, but I've learned a lot about myself these last few months of college, and I respect myself too much to let someone lie to me the way you did."

Shock crosses Becky's face. "You've lost your mind. I'm not a liar."

"Then what exactly *did* happen between you and Matt over the summer?" I watch her closely, intent on catching any sign of dishonesty.

"I told you. We hooked up. Had fun. Now he texts me, wanting more." Not so much as a twitch from her. I don't let the doubt seep into my thoughts like I have in the past.

"That's not what he told me."

Her composed exterior cracks slightly. She turns away from me and looks in the mirror, smoothing her hair. She can't look at me. "And who says he's telling the truth?"

She's so quick to pass blame and hide the truth. How could I have ever believed her?

"He wrote me a letter." I pull it out of the textbook I was using to study and I hold it out in front of me. I know she sees it.

She hesitates. "That doesn't prove anything." I can tell by the way she says it that she's losing steam.

"It proves he cares. He cares for me. He said there was never anything between you, but you wanted there to be."

"He's lying!" She's getting emotional.

I take it one step further. "He said you made a move, and he turned you down. I don't know why I let you get in my head before."

"All right!" she shouts. And then, to my surprise, Becky's shoulders slump and she slowly sits on the edge of her bed. There are tears in her eyes. She's finally cracked.

Ginger and I exchange a look of bewilderment. I decide to do what I would do if I saw anyone crying. I cross the room, hand Becky some tissues, and put my arm around her shoulders. She doesn't push me away. She doesn't yell. She doesn't even speak for a while. She just cries.

"Rejection," she says in a soft voice. "It's the one thing I can't handle. I can't live with it. He chose you over me."

I take my arm off Becky, preparing to listen.

"That first day of school, Matt showed up at our room. I thought he was here to see *me*. I thought he decided he had been wrong, that he wanted to actually be with me. And then he started asking me about *you*. The little blond, wholesome girl—the complete opposite of me. I got angry. Jealous. It was such a slap in the face. He knew I liked him and yet he came into *my* room asking about you."

I honestly can't believe Becky is confessing. "So you made a move."

She wipes a tear from her cheek. "I hung out with him all summer long. All summer. At the end of it, he tells me he doesn't think of me *like that*. Then you come along, meet him for five seconds at a welcome desk, and he comes to find you."

I know it shouldn't make me happy in this weird, uncomfortable moment, but it does. Matt did come looking for me that day. I push down the bubbliness inside so I can focus on listening to Becky. I need to know the whole truth.

"Why would you do that if you knew he didn't want that with you? Were you hoping I'd see you two?" I have to ask. The curiosity is killing me.

She chuckles. It shocks me. "If I'm being completely honest, which it seems I'm being, yeah, I did want you to see us. I was glad you did. I didn't want you to have what I couldn't have."

"Wow. That's..."

"Bitchy?" Becky tries to complete my sentence.

It's my turn to chuckle. "I wasn't going to say exactly that, but that works too."

"You know I wasn't always like this. I was happy-go-lucky like you. Then, when I was sixteen, my dad left one night and never came back. I became bitter. At him, at life, at everything. When I came to PSC and met Matt, I knew he was a good guy. When he told me he wasn't interested, I was heartbroken. Being left, again. Talk about some deep-seated shit, right?"

"I'm sorry about your dad." My head is spinning from all this information. I feel for Becky. I don't know where I'd be without my dad.

"Thanks."

I don't really know what else to say. The moment of silence drags on until Becky begins again. "It hurt seeing you and Matt together that night we all went out. I couldn't believe the way he looked at you. He never looked at me that way. So I got mad and jealous...and I said things to you that weren't true."

"What wasn't true?"

Tears are in Becky's eyes again. "That day we fought...the text from Matt? He texted me asking, no *begging*, me to tell you nothing had happened between us the night before. He wasn't flirting with me or asking to see me again."

I just stood there, absorbing what Becky just said. Matt wasn't with Becky that night. He didn't want to be with her. But just to be sure, I ask Becky, "*Did* anything happen between you two that night?"

Becky stares up at the ceiling, trying to compose herself. "No. After you saw us together, I tried to pull Matt back to keep him from going after you. He told me how much you meant to him. Of course, hearing him say how he felt for you made me even more upset. The next day, well, you know what happened."

I nod slowly. Everything Matt said in the letter was true.

Relief washes over me, in my veins and my heart. I start laughing in what I'm guessing is hysteria. I don't know why. Maybe the absurdity of the whole situation or the relief of knowing this is finally over. I don't have to see Ginger's and Becky's faces to know they are looking at me like I'm crazy.

When my fit of laughter subsides, I turn to Becky. "Can we put all of this behind us?"

"It would be nice to not hold a grudge against my roommate. It was so exhausting."

I smile knowingly at her. It *was* exhausting. "I know we won't be best friends, but I'm glad I know you better now. I think we could be friends."

Becky ponders this. "Friends is a stretch. Let's just get through this year without killing each other."

"Deal. No more being a jerk to me." I point to her.

"I said I'll try my best!"

That was good enough for me.

Ginger pipes up. "So, what are you going to do about Matt?"

"What does she mean?" Becky asks, curious. I eye her, not wanting to upset her but also a little worried she will try to go after Matt again. Sensing this, Becky says, "I'm over Matt! I promise I won't get in your way."

"I've been avoiding him. I didn't know who or what to believe. I didn't want to be a part of the drama."

"I already said I was sorry! I'm not apologizing again."

I roll my eyes at her. Classic Becky.

"What should I do?" I say, looking to my best friend for advice.

"Well, do you like him?" Ginger asks.

"Yes."

"Then you have to go find him and talk."

"I may need your help," I say, turning to Becky, an idea formulating in my head.

"Who, me?" She points to herself, a confused look on her face.

"Yes. I think you owe me, don't you?"

"Fine. But after this, we're even!"

"Deal." We shake on it.

"What are you thinking?" Ginger asks, curiosity clear in her voice.

"You'll see."

DAY 57

CHAPTER 20

─────

The plan is all in place. Becky will convince Matt to meet her for coffee at the student union and I'll do the rest. It was my idea for Becky to be a part of the plan. I know I could have gotten Matt to meet me on his own accord, but I want things to be right between the three of us. Me, Becky, and Matt. No more uncertainty. No more wondering. If she helps me with this, I think Matt will see I've forgiven Becky and she's gotten over the grudge against me. This way he can forgive her too. We all can move on as friends and, hopefully, Matt and I as more.

I sit in the Power PSC studio with my headphones on, waiting for the call to come through.

Ring...ring...ring...

I'm so nervous I drop my phone on the ground. I bend to pick it up and bump my head before answering the call. Before I forget, I mute myself so they won't be able to hear me.

I can hear Matt's voice through the phone. Just as planned.

"Becky, what are we doing here? I already told you I wasn't in the mood for any of your antics." Matt says, sounding defeated. "Black coffee, please." Matt orders his usual.

"Nothing for me, thanks," Becky says to the barista.

"Look, Matt, I just wanted to say I'm sorry. I haven't exactly been a good person these last couple months. I knew you had a thing for Jo and that bothered me. Seeing you with her was hard for me. I was jealous. I know we wouldn't work together but I couldn't help but get in the way."

"Oh, God, Becky, what did you do? Are you the reason why Jo hasn't spoken to me?"

"Hey, I'm trying to make things right here! I may or may not have told Jo you and I hooked up all summer...and I alluded to the fact that you and I spent the night together the night of the party."

"What? How could you do that? You know that's not true! I have to go find her."

"Relax for a second, okay, Lover Boy? I know I've been a bitch in the past, but I'm repenting for my sins. I'm trying to make things right."

"What are you even saying, Becky?"

"Just listen," Becky says. I can tell by the edge of her voice that she's starting to get frustrated.

"No way, I'm done with your games."

"Hey, Dumb-Dumb, just listen, okay?"

That's my cue.

"Hey, PSC, this is Jo Prescott and you're listening to 87.6 FM Power PSC. My time's almost up for today but before I go, I want to dedicate a song to someone very special to me. He's sweet, funny, and also happens to be super hot. I hope you can forgive me. This one's for you." I click "play" and the song we bonded over the very first day hums through the speakers.

I take my headphones off and Jack gives me a thumbs up. We already agreed he'd wrap up things in the studio for me.

"Thanks, Jack!" I rush out of the studio and into the corridor of the student union, searching for Matt.

It's like something out of a movie. Our eyes meet across the crowded room, even though there must be hundreds of people milling about. I pick up my pace and cross the room.

Becky's next to him. A few weeks ago, hell, even a few days ago, this would bother me. But now Becky and I are on good terms.

"I'll leave you two alone," Becky says as she walks away.

We barely notice her leave, too caught up in each other. Being together, both of us knowing that things are finally on the right track—at least that's how I feel. Shit. Will Matt feel the same way? I didn't really have time to think about what would happen if he was over me.

I can't wait any longer. "Hey." I'm nervous. I'm excited. What is he thinking?

"You played our song."

My heart squeezes when he says "our" song. I have the biggest smile stretching across my face.

"You didn't think it was cheesy?"

"I like cheesy." He looks around, seemingly noticing the crowds of people for the first time. Maybe this isn't the best place for our private conversation. He takes my hand and leads me outside. We sit on a bench under a tree on the student union lawn.

It's a chilly December day, and there's fresh snow on the ground, but I don't feel cold at all. I can feel the blood coursing through my veins. I feel alive, like I usually do when I'm with Matt.

"So...you think I'm super hot?" Matt smiles.

"Did I say that?"

"Yeah, with plenty of conviction, might I add."

"I can't believe that's what you're focusing on." I roll my eyes at him, playfully.

"I'm only teasing. No girl has ever given me such a romantic gesture."

"I guess I'm not like other girls."

"No, you're definitely not. I knew that from the moment I met you." Matt puts his hands on either side of my face and I forget to breathe temporarily. "You're one of a kind, Jo Prescott." He leans in and his lips are on mine. For the first time in a month, I feel complete. My body tingles at his touch, and I feel the heat rising inside me. I've missed this. I've missed him.

After I don't know how long, we pull apart. "Wow, I guess you really liked my speech, huh?"

Matt starts laughing. "It was okay, I guess."

I punch him lightly in the shoulder.

"I'm kidding! I loved it. So, you forgive me for not telling you the truth sooner?"

"Yes. I loved your letter by the way. Do you forgive me for blowing you off that night after the party?"

"Yes. I still don't understand, though. Why didn't you meet me?"

"The short answer is Becky. The long answer is that I didn't know what or who to believe. Becky told me one thing and you told me another. I think the cynical part of me didn't want to believe you were telling the truth. How could someone like you want to be with someone like me and not Becky? She's everything I'm not."

"Exactly. You're everything she's not. You're everything I want in a girl. Smart, funny, kind, and I'll use your words: super hot. Sure, Becky is attractive in her own way, but in my eyes, she's nothing compared to you. When I make you smile or laugh, it's such a rush. I want to make you happy."

I blush at his words. "You do make me happy. Especially when you give me all these compliments."

"Oh, do you want me to keep going? You have a voice for radio, but definitely not a face for radio." He winks at me and, as corny as this all seems, I can't wipe the stupid grin off my face.

"Okay, stop, stop. Now you're just buttering me up."

"I'm just complimenting my girl."

"You're a dork, but you're *my* dork."

"If anyone is a dork, it's you!"

"I won't argue with that. We can both be dorks."

"As long as we're together."

DAY 75

CHAPTER 21

I'm sitting in my psych final and fill in the last bubble on the scantron. Around me are other students with their heads down, pencils moving back and forth. I raise my hand, waiting for one of the TAs to collect my test papers. One of them, who I'm very familiar with, comes over and looks over my test to make sure all of my information is filled out and checks that my student ID matches what I wrote down. She gives me a thumbs up and whispers so as to not disturb the other students. "You're free to go. Have a great winter vacation!"

"Thank you!" I whisper back, gathering my things and heading outside.

It's a brisk day at PSC but I can't help but pause for a moment outside the testing center to take a deep breath and let it sink in that my first college semester is over. I can't believe it.

I text Ginger.

Text me when you're done with the psych final!

I put my phone away and begin my walk to the coffee shop that Matt and I would go to after class. He promised to meet me there after my final.

It's been quiet on campus this week since some students have already left for the semester, so I don't see as many people around as I normally do and it's a strange feeling.

My phone vibrates, breaking me from my thoughts. It's from Ginger.

DONE!

I text back.

"Let's go to the dining hall. I'm hungry."

Ginger responds in seconds.

See you there! I'll bring Peyton!

I push the coffee shop door open and find Matt sitting at a table reading a book. He's so damn cute.

I skip up to him and put my finger under his chin to tilt his face up to see mine. "Hi, handsome. What are you reading?"

Matt smiles and closes his book. He pulls me onto his lap and kisses my cheek. When he does cute things like this, my heart melts. "I was just pretending so you'd think I was an intellectual." He tightens his imaginary tie and I giggle. "So, how was the test?"

"I think it went pretty well. I can't believe I'm done! One semester down, seven to go. It feels like it went by so slow but also so fast. I don't know how to explain it."

"I get what you mean."

"I'm meeting Ginger and Peyton for lunch. You want to come?"

"Somewhere with food? I'm in." Matt sets me on the floor, and we intertwine our hands. Sometimes I still can't believe we're together.

On our walk to the dining hall, I spot Becky. "Hey, Becky!" Matt and I walk over to her. Becky and I have been on pretty good terms ever since our heart-to-heart and the fact that she helped me get Matt back. I think she's been seeing someone, because she's been in an unusually good mood lately.

"Hey, guys, what are you up to?"

Who would have thought the three of us would be here today having such a casual conversation?

"Going to lunch. Do you want to come?" It's funny we're at a point where I wouldn't find it weird to get a meal with Becky and Matt together. If you told me a month ago, I would have laughed in your face.

"Thanks for the offer, but I'm actually off to my last final. Wish me luck!"

"Good luck!" Matt and I say together.

"Stop being so cute, it's sickening," Becky says over her shoulder with a true look of disgust on her face. I guess not everything is perfect, but what can you do?

Matt and I make it to the dining hall and I immediately spot Ginger's purple hair and Peyton's curls.

"You guys already got food?" I say, pretending to be offended.

Ginger shrugs her shoulders. "You took too long! You know I can't resist food if it's mere feet away. But I did make sure to get you some fries, so you're welcome."

"You do know me!" I go over and squeeze Ginger and Peyton in a tight embrace.

"Okay, Jo, eat your fries and let us eat in peace without you cutting off our circulation."

Peyton scracks up and once he's done, he says, "Man, I don't think I'll ever get tired of Ginger's attitude."

Ginger blushes. It's still weird for me to see her so smitten.

"So, can you believe it? We're done with first semester! Now we get a nice long winter break." As happy as I am, I'm a little bummed I won't be able to spend it all with Matt.

Luckily, we don't live far from each other at home, so we'll still hang out. Maybe we'll go into NYC to see the Christmas lights.

"I plan to spend as much time as I can on the slopes. Shredding the gnar." Peyton gives us the hang loose sign.

"I'm finally going to Thailand to visit my sister," Ginger says with a big smile on her face.

"You must be so excited to see her!" I can't hide my enthusiasm. She's literally talked about this since the first day I met her.

"Sure, but think about all the food I'm going to eat!"

"I should have known that's what you'd be excited about."

"What are you guys up to? Eating all the New York-style pizza you can?" Peyton asks in a teasing tone.

I stick my tongue out at him for good measure. "We're not having this debate again! New York-style pizza is the best, end of story. I'm just happy to go home and relax with my family for the holidays and hopefully hang out with this guy." I snuggle my head into Matt's shoulder.

"What about you, Matt?" Ginger asks through a mouth full of french fries.

"I usually help my parents cook a big Italian Christmas Eve dinner, and that takes at least three days to prep. After that, I'll probably be recovering from all the food."

"That sounds amazing. Can you cook for us next semester?" Ginger asks excitedly.

I look around at my group of friends and can't help but smile. This semester has been such a roller coaster, yet here I am at the end of it, wondering how it's over already. I had a toxic relationship with my roommate that I mended, I met my best friend Ginger, I found Hot Boy Matt, who is now my boyfriend, and I discovered my interest in radio.

"Jo? Hello! Why is this girl always zoning out?" Ginger chuckles.

If only they knew! "What did I miss?"

"We're going for coffee. You in?"

"I'll walk with you guys there. I have to do my last shift at the station in ten minutes."

I hug Ginger and Peyton goodbye and give Matt a kiss on the cheek. I head toward the radio station, but I feel a hand pull me back.

"Not so fast." Matt pulls me in for a real kiss. When we finally come up for air, I'm dizzy.

"Are you trying to distract me before my show?"

Matt laughs. "Something like that. See you later, 409." He winks at me, and my heart skips a beat. I love my nickname.

I blow him a kiss and head to the station.

* * *

"Hey, PSC, this is Jo Prescott and you're listening to 87.6 FM Power PSC. Today is the last day of finals, so if you're listening to this now, you are either about to be done with fall semester or *you are done*! Congrats! Can't wait to be back on air with you all in the spring. Have a great winter break!"

I turn off my mic for the last time this semester, happier and more confident than I was just a mere three months ago. PSC has become my home and I wouldn't want it any other way.

ACKNOWLEDGMENTS

This book would not have been possible without my amazing beta readers. Your support means the world to me. Thank you to for making *75 Days of Jo* a reality!

Alec Broniszewski

Alex Paradero

Alex Walsh

Alison Matuszewski

Aly Motter

Alyssa Mortillaro

Amber Kloper

Amy Hilty

Andrew Shemick

Anjana Sreedhar

Anna Vorse

Brandon Posivak

Bret Pontillo

Brittney Merrigan

Carly Herrera

Caroline Russo

Catie & Tyler Ball

Chris McGann

Christian Castelli

Concetta Heffernan

Dane & Jeannine Iovino

Daniel Andrus

Danielle Barnes

Danielle Diaz-Albertini

David Contino

David Sperber

Debra Contino

Dona Rozsypal

Dustin Soliven

Eileen Gilbert

Elizabeth Mabery

Elizabeth Mahoney

Emma Gilbert

Eric Hirsh

Eric Koester
Erin Bodine
Gaby Gladfelter
Gail Williams
Harriet McCarter
Honey Daengdej
James McCarter
Jasmine Chou
Jenna Wecht
Jennifer Camisa
Jim Canfield
Jim Johnson
Jo-Ann Basile
John McCarter
Jordan Malmed
Justin Mortensen
Kaity Gonzalez
Kat Ogden
Katie Gnatt
Katie McCarter
Katrina Koch
Keith & Amy Heffernan
Kelly Gilbert
Kelly McCarter
Lamar Smith
Lauren Doberstein
Lexy Smyles
Linda McCarter
Lucas Pontillo
Mai Foringer
Maria Sarubbi
Marial Giuliano

Marissa Faas
Matthew Jentis
Megan Escobar
Melissa Montano
Michelle Williams
Miranda Sheaffer
Morgan Williams
Ozlem Serif
Patricia Pontillo
Paul & Carmela Rozsypal
Paul & Mia Rozsypal
Peter & Lynne Pontillo
Philip John Basile
Phuong Vu
Rachel Pontillo
Rachael Mesibov
Rachel Perini
Rachel Rodriguez
Rachel Stanford
Rebecca McGowan
Rick McDermott
Samantha Alpert
Samantha Brodsky
Samantha Stauffer
Sarah Herguth
Sarah Kegerreis
Sarah Van Alstyne
Scott Mayr
Sean Campbell
Sean Sullivan
Soufieh Hakimzadeh
Steven Mezzacappa